JUDICIOUS DISCIPLINE

REVISED FIFTH EDITION

Forrest Gathercoal

JUDICIOUS DISCIPLINE
By Forrest Gathercoal
Revised Fifth Edition

Library of Congress Cataloging-in-Publication Data

Gathercoal, Forrest.
   Judicious discipline / Forrest Gathercoal.-- Rev. 5th ed.
     p. cm.
   Includes bibliographical references (p.).
   ISBN 1-880192-39-X (alk. paper)
    1. School discipline--United States. 2. Classroom management--United States. 3.
Students--Legal status, laws, etc.--United States. I. Title.

LB3011 .G35 2001
371.02'4--dc21

2001040765

CONTENTS

⚖️

Notes:

ACKNOWLEDGMENTS

he concepts and practice of *Judicious Discipline* have now evolved into this Fifth Edition with the help and support of many educators. I have not forgetten those who assisted on the first four editions, and would like to recognize them again for having faith in my ideas. I will always appreciate the help of Barbara McEwan and Kenneth Ahrendt for their editorial assistance; Barbara McEwan and Robert Bolden for their research; Margaret Abbott, Dan Anstine, Jerry Balaban, Glenn Gwynn, Kenneth Haines, Ken Hill, Richard Jensen, Paula Kinney, Jan Knight, Steve Mathews, Robert O'Neill, and Robert Payne for their consultative assistance; Lucy Senter for her secretarial support; and my dean, Robert Barr, for his continued help and encouragement.

For the Third Edition, I wish to gratefully acknowledge and express my appreciation to Michelle Comeaux, Paul Gathercoal, Jim Holden, John Horn, Richard Jensen, Mike Mangan, Barbara McEwan, and Ken Winograd. These dedicated educators have provided me the candid feedback and editorial help that I needed to go to the next level.

The Fourth Edition has been fleshed out and polished with three more years of feedback from countless educators and friends. I would like to add to the above list Virginia Nimmo,

Nancy Busse, Julie Rae Petersen, Louise and Vern Jones, Jay Casbon, and my incredible brother Paul Gathercoal.

This fifth edition has been enriched primarily by the research of Paul Gathercoal and Virginia Nimmo and Paul's ideas on class meetings.

To my publisher Alan H. Jones at Caddo Gap Press, thanks for believing in these ideas and for all your help throughout these five editions.

And finally, to my wonderful wife Joan, son Bob, daughter Sue, teachers, students, and friends who have shared their lives with me—thanks for being there.

—Forrest Gathercoal

PREFACE

judicious...1. having or exercising sound judgment...2. directed or governed by sound usu. dispassionate judgement; character-ized by discretion...**syn**. see **wise**.

—Webster's Third New International Dictionary

discipline...1. a branch of knowledge or learning...2. training that develops self-control, character, or orderliness and effi-ciency...3. self-control or orderly conduct...4. a system of rules...5. treatment that corrects.

—Webster's New World Dictionary

A n uncomplicated, yet workable, rule has evolved from the classrooms of successful teachers throughout our country that simply states, "You may do what you want in this classroom until it interferes with the rights of others." It is a teacher's way of acknowledging individual differences among students while recognizing the need for an educational environment free from disruptive forces. Educators applying this philoso-phy in an evenhanded manner to student conduct are unknow-ingly teaching and respecting their students' constitutional

9

rights. At the same time, teachers are creating classroom environments in which students are able to learn about and experience their responsibilities for the other members of the class.

The ideas set forth are fashioned upon ethical, educational, and legal perspectives for school rules and decisions based on America's democratic form of government. ***Judicious Discipline*** creates a democratic management style that serves as a real-life model for the same system of rules and responsibilities under which students will live when they leave school.

This book was written for educators whose goal is to educate students capable of living responsibly in a free nation that holds high the constitutional principles of freedom, justice, and equality. These democratic principles, balanced with the welfare needs of others, can be judiciously woven into the traditional values that schools have historically passed along to their students.

Judicious Discipline is also about educational practices that teach students many personal qualities, such as accountability, self-efficacy, tolerance, cooperation, and mutual respect.

Six Chapters

This book is divided into six chapters:

Chapter 1—**Introduction to Judicious Discipline** sets out the rationale for a democratic school community as opposed to an autocratic environment. It contrasts an intrinsic "judicious" approach to discipline with methods that employ an extrinsic model of rewards and punishments.

Chapter 2—**Professional Ethics** functions as the conscience of good educational practices. This chapter examines professional ethics and recommends strategies designed to create and maintain a professional relationship that is always working in students' best interests.

Chapter 3—**A Constitutional Perspective for School Rules** is a review of the legal principles applicable to creating and maintaining a democratic school environment. It is the foundation of and serves as the framework for educators to help their students understand the implementation of fair rules and decisions in schools today.

Chapter 4—**The Democratic Classroom Community** describes how to organize a democratic school community. Although students will learn as "student/citizens" that they have freedom to be themselves within the classroom, they also will learn about the responsibilities that accompany those freedoms.

Chapter 5—**Consequences—a Professional Relationship Model** introduces a mentoring approach for resolving problems that focuses on strategies for helping students learn and recover from their misbehavior. This chapter also serves as a guide for the establishment of judicious consequences designed to keep intact a student/educator relationship of trust and care.

Chapter 6—**Balancing Rights and Responsibilities** provides a resource for educators about what rights students have in public schools and how to balance them with their responsibilities for the welfare of the school community. This chapter is not meant to be all inclusive of disciplinary issues facing educators, but it does contain many representative examples of school management practices that affect student rights and responsibilities in public schools today.

In summary, ***Judicious Discipline*** is written for educators who want to break away from an autocratic management style and establish a democratic school community. It is a philosophy that establishes a professional relationship model for handling student misbehavior designed to replace rewards and punishments commonly used in autocratic classrooms. Guided by sound ethical, educational, and democratic principles, students in democratic classrooms are learning the self-discipline necessary to resolve for themselves problems presented in the normal course of classroom living. As a consequence, educators will be helping students develop a more principled level of intellectual and moral development.

CHAPTER 1

INTRODUCTION TO JUDICIOUS DISCIPLINE

One of my first assignments as a beginning teacher was supervising an after-game dance. I had not been to a high school dance for a number of years, and therefore was somewhat surprised by the way students were dancing. The only lighting in the gym came from the four exit signs above the doorways.

In almost complete darkness, students seemed fused together as they barely moved to the very slow music being played. Because no one seemed concerned about this type of dancing in the dark, I quickly adapted and engaged in conversation with the other chaperons under one of the exit lights.

However, three weeks later, when I was again assigned to dance duty, I walked into a fully lighted gymnasium filled with the sounds of upbeat music. The students were trying to do a new dance they called "The Twist." Some of the girls had seen it on television and were teaching the others how to do it. Most were not very good at doing these gyrations, but they seemed to be really enjoying trying something different.

Shortly after I arrived, the principal walked in and was visibly

13

shaken by this new dance. He told us that he was offended by the movements of the hips and likened it to a simulation of sexual intercourse. He stopped the music immediately and proceeded to ban The Twist from all school dances. The disappointed students turned out the lights, put on the slow music, and went back to the "school-approved" close dancing.

About twenty years later, my son attended his first junior high dance, where all the students were doing The Twist and other similar dances popular at the time. He told me that one of the girls at the dance put on a slow record, turned down the lights a bit, and began teaching everyone a new dance. She called it "close dancing," where boys and girls would hold each other as they danced together slowly. You guessed it. The principal came in, found the students holding on to each other, and banned "close dancing" at the school. So they turned up the lights, put on the rock music, and returned to the style of dancing that I had seen banned twenty years before.

Many of us have been in education long enough to experience some school rules coming full circle. Being fair and consistent is extremely important to the integrity of the rules and decisions we make, yet very difficult to achieve over the long haul. Because of a constant parade of new fads and changing lifestyles, educators must rely on basic guidelines that will avoid visceral and capricious reactions to every new situation that comes along. The solution, therefore, lies in maintaining guiding principles that will withstand the test of time.

This statement, of course, begs the question—what are these guiding principles? The answer is found in the constitutional tenets upon which all our nation's laws have been established; **individual freedom, justice, and equality balanced with the welfare needs and interests of society**. These time-tested principles have sustained our country for over two centuries and now can be used as a basis for learning and behavioral expectations for students in school. The integration of these principles of civility into daily practices of educators is the focus of this book.

This principled level of ethical reasoning gives students a common structure for understanding individual discretion while still providing adequate guidelines of acceptable social interaction. As interactions between students and educators are based on this more abstract sense of responsibility, they move beyond rewards and punishment to an understanding of human responsibility reflecting a higher level of moral development.

Trying to remember "all the rules" is much more difficult than accepting and abiding by a moral and ethical code of relatively few principles from which all interactions would flow. A democratic classroom community acting positively toward one another within the structure of these guiding principles creates a freedom of movement that brings forth qualities such as confidence, trust, and conscientiousness.

Practice, patience, and principled leadership are required on the part of educators as students learn to incorporate the abstract concepts of social responsibility into their behavior. For example, most of us can quite easily get a fix on the rule "Never cheat on a test." But a more principled approach would be to help students understand the morality issues surrounding the concept of truth and learn to live with the ambiguity of the many questions that arise from the more abstract principle "Be true to yourself and others."

Judicious Discipline is a management style based on the synthesis of professional ethics, good educational practice, and students' constitutional rights and responsibilities. It is a philosophy that uses rules and consequences to build an educational community designed to keep students in school, rather than push them out. Educators have always believed students should take responsibly for their actions and that teaching citizenship is an important part of any curriculum. ***Judicious Discipline***, however, takes that belief one step further—it provides a framework and the language for educators to create an environment that respects the citizenship rights of students. As a result, students will be learning and experiencing a model of discipline that emphasizes personal responsibility.

A democratic community does not mean students vote on every decision or that the majority rules in every situation. On the contrary, a school community that practices democracy is one where educators teach and model principles of civility as the foundation for personal growth and interactions among its members. It is a school in which individual differences are respected and students feel they have value as citizen/students. The constitutional framework ensures an atmosphere of civil morality that cuts across the many cultural, ethnic, and religious traditions represented by the diversity of family values children bring with them to school.

A democratic school community sends its members a powerful message that their human rights are secure. One of the primary reasons students misbehave in schools is due to feeling insecure because they mistakenly believe they are not being accepted for who they are. As they subconsciously compensate for this sense of vulnerability, their behavior moves them away from the community. Students can express these insecurities outwardly by becoming very disruptive to everyone around them, or express them inwardly by giving up on themselves.

It is also found that in dysfunctional situations where personal and societal boundaries are not respected, students have the feeling they are not "whole." When personal identity is blurred by co-dependency, students become dysfunctional and find the "system" very controlling. Therefore, as students learn the concept of "boundaries," both those of society as well as their individual capabilities, it has the effect of affirming their unique qualities and autonomous rights.

The real issue is how a democratic management style influences students to believe they have a valued place in the school community. In a school environment in which students do not have to continually prove their worth, they experience real feelings of belonging. Regardless of their background, abilities, and behavior, they are accepted and made to feel they have permanent value. Insecurities are then replaced with concern for others, feelings of self-worth and confidence, a sense of belonging, and a cooperative attitude.

Ultimately, the practice of democratic principles guides students toward understanding and accepting a social contract of mutual responsibility. In democratic classrooms, responsibility flows from a principled level of thinking where students learn to balance their human rights with the welfare interests of the school community. On the other hand, autocratic classrooms do not recognize rights, but think in terms of "student privileges," usually equating responsibility with obedience. There is something anomalous about the phrase "student rights and obedience," but that is what autocratic educators typically mean when they give lip-service to student rights.

But educators who respect human rights and teach students about our nation's civil morality are giving new meaning and real substance to the phrase **student rights and responsibilities**. Students are learning that with power comes social responsibility.

Problems with Rewards and Punishments

Alvin Toffler in his book *Powershifts* discusses three types of power: knowledge, wealth, and violence. Violence, he states, is the lowest form of power because it is finite and its effect is lessened when the other side has it. Money is also finite as its influence decreases as the other side uses it. Additionally, some students simply cannot be scared or bought off. Knowledge is the highest form of power, because it is infinite and its effectiveness increases as the other side possesses it and all rational people respond to it. If, in fact, rewards (wealth) and punishment (violence) are finite, educators using these strategies will one day become powerless in their educational settings. And yet many educators continue to use a system of rewards and punishments designed to motivate and control students.

The argument goes that once the rules and consequences are established, educators must be consistent as they play out their predetermined plan of action. Furthermore, autocratic educators are convinced that bending the rules might lead to greater problems or that treating one student differently would not be fair to the others. The point is often made that students know what the rules are and should not be surprised or even upset over paying the consequences for their wrongdoings. This line of reasoning leads to the conclusion that punishment is what adults will experience in the "real world" and that the fear of punishment will, in the long run, teach responsibility.

Punishment at first appears to be just and logical and usually has immediate results. Upon closer scrutiny, however, punishing students usually has the opposite effect from the one intended. If misbehaving students already suffer from feelings of insecurity, then punishing them only confirms their sense of inadequacy. They feel themselves being pushed further away from the community and often develop a siege mentality to defend their sense of humanity. Punishment by definition is designed to make students feel more insecure and, as a result, always makes situations worse.

Punishment leaves students hating and fearing educators. They respond by lying, cheating, withdrawing, and often becoming nonparticipants in school activities. Most students who feel they are being punished, regardless of the educator's intent, believe they have license to reciprocate by wanting to do something to punish the educator back. This retaliatory urge stifles any constructive communication and often is the beginning of an adversarial relationship. The result is that students feel pushed away from educators, often turning to others less able to help them work through their problems or to people who do not have their best interests in mind.

Whereas helpful feedback and positive reinforcement is designed to strengthen a desired behavior, punishment has the effect of suppressing an undesired behavior. For example, if teachers want to encourage their students to feel free to express opinions in class, they should avoid putting down student complaints about homework assignments with remarks such as, "All you do is complain in this class. Why don't you grow up and learn to be responsible."

To many teachers, such a demeaning statement would appear to be an appropriate way of making the point that complaining in class is not responsible behavior. But from the student's perspective, it is a message that the act of expressing opinions may result in being publicly embarrassed as well as not always being positively reinforced in the classroom.

On the other hand, an approach using reflective feedback might have the teacher respond by saying something like, "I'm glad you spoke up because I didn't realize that you might be having some problems with homework. Let's talk privately to see what we can work out." If educators would avoid remarks designed to shame students and go immediately to the real issues, in this case encouraging expression of opinions as well as identifying problems with homework, a safe atmosphere for personal growth is established.

External rewards also create a number of problems. Rewarding students, for example, has the effect of extinguishing their behaviors. In other words, when the rewards stop, so does the behavior. Rewards have a way of putting a market value on student/educator relationships by attempting to buy desired behavior. Stickers used to motivate young students, for example, are finite and will have to get bigger and better as students get older in order to continue motivating student interest, while learning activities will illicit little more than a "what's in it for me" attitude.

In addition, external rewards and punishments create a co-dependent relationship between students and educators. This means that students' every thought and act plays off the teacher, by either behaving in ways that will be rewarded, or fearing some sort of punishment for their actions. For example, students who do their homework only for the reward of a grade or fear what will happen to them if they do not, are not really learning the educational value of homework or experiencing the intrinsic rewards of being responsible for their own learning.

Students who grow up making decisions in order to please teachers or to avoid punishment or to receive a reward tend to lead very stressful lives. This constant dependency on approval usually discourages students from thinking responsibly for themselves and learning to act independently. Educators who use bribery are sending a message that they do not trust the cognitive abilities of students and, as a result, further discourage accountability. By teaching students the language of respecting others as they would be treated, it eliminates the need for approval as a motivator.

In the final analysis, students who feel they are not being justly rewarded, or who are punished by their teachers for any reason, are angered and feel like reciprocating in kind. As a result, educators manipulating their students with rewards and punishments simply create no-win situations that severely strain a professional relationship. All too often the outcome is either a fearful, dependent, and obedient student, or an adversary in search of a "power struggle."

Implementation

Judicious Discipline is not intended to be used independently, but as a scaffold for other cognitive strategies and ideas. Because it is designed as a framework, other cognitive management techniques must also be employed in order to meet the needs of all students.

Many educators, however, already use many of these methods that fit very well with *Judicious Discipline*. Educators employing teaching strategies such as cooperative learning and whole language, for example, will find it very easy to integrate *Judicious Discipline*'s philosophy and language into their daily practices. The real world practicality of cooperation in a learning environment and the democratic nature of whole language fit logically with what students are experiencing through *Judicious Discipline*.

In addition to academic strategies, educators who have been employing Rudolph Dreikurs' Social Discipline have been using strategies designed to take over exactly where *Judicious Discipline* leaves off. *Judicious Discipline* provides the language of a democratic community which has always been the centerpiece of Dreikurs' work.

In the area of moral development, Harvard psychologist Lawrence Kohlberg has described five stages. Stage 1 (punishment) and Stage 2 (rewards) respond to personal needs and others' rules. Stage 3 (good boy/good girl) and Stage 4 (law and order) are based on the approval of others. But Stage 5 (social contract theory) is moral development determined by socially agreed upon standards of individual rights, a civil morality similar to that of the U.S. Constitution. Because the first four stages depend on the approval of others, they are extrinsic

motivators and designed to teach obedience. Not until students
are at Stage 5 of moral development will their behavior become
intrinsic and will they learn to make responsible decisions. Until
students have something to be responsible for (individual rights),
they will not learn responsibility, only obedience. *Judicious
Discipline* is the language and model for students and educators
to achieve a school environment at Stage 5 of moral development.

Educators who have used student-centered methods of teaching seem to move quite comfortably to the concepts of *Judicious
Discipline*. The model not only reinforces their present practices by giving them a language to support what they have been
doing already, but gives them more ideas to progress even
further towards building a democratic community. These educators have found it helpful to continue reading *Judicious Discipline* as well as work with the examples and lesson plans in
*Practicing Judicious Discipline: An Educator's Guide to a Demo-
cratic Classroom*, edited by Barbara McEwan. For school support
staff and volunteers, I have written a book entitled *A Judicious
Philosophy for School Support Personnel*, which enables them to
become familiar with and reinforce the *Judicious Discipline*
approach used in schools and classrooms. Also available is my
Judicious Parenting, written especially for parents whose children are in democratic classrooms and who would like to use the
same principles of civility to create a democratic family community of their own. In addition, there is a 25-minute videotape
which we created at Oregon State University introducing the
concept of *Judicious Discipline* as well as a videotape on
conducting democratic class meetings by Paul Gathercoal. (All of
these materials are cited in the Bibliography of Resources and
References.)

Many educators who have familiarized themselves with the
concepts of *Judicious Discipline* start right off on the first day
of class by involving their students in setting up a democratic
classroom. They begin with a discussion of student rights,

develop rules together based on student responsibilities flowing from those rights, and discuss with students the process of how things will be handled when they act irresponsibly. Most of the teachers who begin this way have already been doing much the same thing in their classroom, but without the language and structure *Judicious Discipline* provides. Other teachers, however, feel better starting slowly by introducing some of the language and empowering strategies suggested in the text.

It is important to note, however, that if educators do not sincerely believe students have the ability to think and behave responsibly, a democratic environment simply will not work for them. In addition to trust, students must be taught the language of civil rights and responsibilities and these principles must be modeled by educators. Regardless of how educators initiate *Judicious Discipline*, their success is directly related to their ability to trust students, teaching them the concepts of rights and responsibilities, and acting in ways consistent with civil responsibility. To teach one thing and do another is an abuse of power and is disrespectful to the human rights of the students.

Difficulties and Limitations

Building a democratic school community is not always easy. Most of us grew up in autocratic classrooms taught by well-meaning teachers doing what they believed to be their best under varying circumstances. Teachers who were fair, firm, and used appropriate punishments gave most of us a feeling of comfort and security. All we had to do was learn to obey them. If we were caught disobeying, we could, perhaps, find something cleansing about suffering through a well-intentioned punishment.

When we became teachers ourselves, the "boss" approach is

how many of us honestly believed classrooms should be managed. An autocratic approach appeared preferable because problems were handled quickly and they were soon out of the way. In addition, most of us in education have succeeded in an autocratic school system. "After all," we may occasionally think to ourselves, "I turned out all right." Even as adults today, many of us still seek out the security of boundaries drawn by others.

As a result of these factors, changing to a democratic school community takes time to process new perceptions and expectations on the part of both students and educators. Often teachers expect too much too quickly. They think that with the presentation of democratic concepts and some discussion, students will immediately know how to handle their freedom and accompanying responsibilities. We must not forget, however, that students come into their classes having experienced years of autocratic environments and are "wired" to expect to be told what to do. Add to that the variables of maturation, personality development, and the fact that learning and personal growth are always gradual, and it is easy to understand why a democratic community takes some time to establish. Too often educators make the mistake of using an autocratic approach in an attempt to create a democratic school environment.

Even beyond the difficulties of changing management styles, there are limitations to any approach educators use for classroom discipline—and *Judicious Discipline* is no exception. There are, for example, always some students who are emotionally unstable or who suffer from physiological disorders whom cognitive methods will not affect immediately. When this occurs, or when students get completely out of control, other resources have to be brought into play.

But with these limitations, and the many intrinsic difficulties of a paradigm shift, one of the appealing qualities of *Judicious Discipline* is that it does not intensify the problem or "add insult to injury." There is a healing nature inherent in the principles of

24

our nation's Constitution from which "good vibes" and mutual respect seem to emanate. As a result, ***Judicious Discipline*** works to minimize classroom stress and anxiety for both students and teachers because of the environmental emphasis on human rights and individual dignity. Students who are consistently treated with respect at school will eventually begin looking at themselves that way. If students are going to develop feelings of autonomy and self-efficacy, they need an environment where they can practice the responsibility that comes with being themselves.

I would like to end this introductory chapter with something that helped me through the throes of my early teaching experience. It is a quote from the psychologist Alfred Adler, whose writings have been very influential in the development of my professional practices and of the concepts set forth in this book. He wrote, "We are concerned not with the possession of truth, but the struggle for it."

When I first began teaching, I remember at the time how concerned I was with the possession of truth because I mistakenly believed at the time that there were "truths" to becoming a good educator. It was not until much later that I discovered I should have learned to appreciate and enjoy more the "struggle of teaching."

Hopefully the ideas in ***Judicious Discipline*** will do just that for those who read it. We should learn to enjoy our students. And on our good days, when we can, we should learn to revel in the "struggle."

Notes:

CHAPTER 2:
PROFESSIONAL
ETHICS

rofessional ethics are the conscience of a school community; they serve as acceptable standards of moral and
proper conduct. Ethics are sometimes referred to as "beginning where the law stops." For example, there is no law
against a teacher confronting a student with, "Why can't you be
as good as your sister was in this class?" But viewed through
professional ethics, the comparing of students is considered poor
educational practice, one that will often precipitate attitudinal
problems that negatively affect the level of student achievement.

The foundation of professional ethics lies in the manifestation
of educators always **acting in the best interests of their
students**. For example, misbehaving students sitting alone in
hallways can seldom see the logic of how isolation is helping them
resolve the matter in question. It is hard for students to believe
that educators who take these kinds of actions are really on their
side and not their adversary acting to push them away from the
school community. As a result, educators must avoid saying and
doing things that cause students to feel outside; they must
instead establish a professional relationship that welcomes and

serves. The lifeblood of an ethical relationship lies in students believing that **their** best interests are foremost in the minds of their educators.

There is often a difference between what one says is the ethical thing to do and what one actually does when a problem presents itself. When an ethical dilemma actually occurs, it is often complicated by time constraints, unforeseen situational factors, and emotions that are not present when a person reasons abstractly about a hypothetical course of moral action. As a result, until educators are put under pressure to act, they are never really sure how they will behave. The ethics educators espouse, therefore, must be practiced over and over so that students will feel secure knowing what they can expect. Over a period of time, students will gain confidence and come to believe that educators will always be acting in their best interests.

Student-Centered

For centuries, educators have argued the merits of two educational theories. The theory of child depravity held the child to be **evil** at birth, and it stressed that corruptive weakness could be corrected only by a strong teacher who used authoritarian methods. In contrast, the naturalistic educators believed that the child was innately **good**. Concerned with examining the child's nature, they believed that the stages of human growth and development provided clues for appropriate educational methods. These educators emphasized "learning by doing" and interaction with the environment.

This age-old question of whether students are inherently "good" or "evil" can be used as one factor for determining professional ethics and responsibilities. For example, educators who think students are inherently "good" believe they can trust students. They are quite comfortable putting into practice methods designed to help students learn and develop attitudes of respect and responsibility. The professional ethics of these educators will usually reflect a **student-centered** approach to educating students. Student-centered educators respond to troubled students by focusing on what happened and what needs to be done. These educators will empower students by saying such things as, "Tell me about it," and "What do you think needs to be learned here?" Every interaction with misbehaving students centers on the resolution of the problem by creating learning experiences that allow them to grow and recover from mistakes. It is this growth that results in learning responsibility.

Conversely, educators who believe students are naturally "evil" will tend not to trust students' ability to think and act responsibly. As a result, these educators feel they must use their power to control students through rules and consequences designed to coerce and "keep em' in line." These autocratic educators are more **educator-centered** as they define their professional ethics.

Educator-centered educators are likely to respond to troubled students by focusing more on the student. These educators exert their authority by saying such things as, "If your homework is not in on time, it will be graded down," as well as responding to student inquiries with statements like, "Because I am your teacher and I told you to, that's why."

Often viewed as evil, troublesome students tend to be perceived as "real problems" because they are not only annoying, but also intrusive, since time and energy have to be devoted to dealing with their misbehavior. This is not to say, however, that all educator-centeredness is based on the belief that all students are evil.

Educator-centered educators, consciously or unconsciously, feel they need to **exert their power** for the purpose of creating obedient students. The result is a compounding of the problem.

29

By establishing and keeping their power, usually through a system of rewards and punishments, these educators are passing these demanding and authoritative attitudes on to their students. Their students in turn then use these same practices to exert power back at their teachers. The result will be power struggles—the single most difficult problem teachers face in maintaining classroom discipline.

Student-centeredness, on the other hand, should be viewed by educators as an opportunity to **share their power and authority**. By empowering students they trust with cognitive skills and authority to make their own decisions, educators are helping them to think independently and act responsibly. By the same token, educators who model an attitude of responsibility for helping students grow and develop instill in them the values of cooperation and mutual respect. Because of the broad difference between the ethics of the two approaches, educators who are successful in creating democratic school communities, by definition, must be student-centered in their educational ethics.

For educators to become student-centered, there must be a style and technique developed to communicate the drama and art of professional responsibility. This is characterized by an ability to transcend daily interactions with students through a communication that begins by getting the "Personal Self" out of the way. Getting one's self-consciousness out of the way, however, is very difficult to do.

By minimizing self-consciousness and emphasizing educational responsibilities, educators will experience a feeling of being more in tune with students' problems and less concerned with themselves. For example, an educator who is aware of a student living in an abusive home is more likely to have a tolerant and helpful attitude toward the student's disruptive behavior in school because the teacher will not view the misbehavior as directed at the teacher or the school. This emphasis on differences among students, combined with a sense of professional responsibility, has a way of overshadowing educator's personal biases and self-interests.

With practice, educators can develop a "mindset of professional responsibility" in which behavior problems are relatively unimportant compared to the educational and developmental needs of students. If every thought and act play off the importance of maintaining the trust and care indispensable to a strong professional relationship, the question asked again and again becomes: **how would a student-centered educator act upon this matter**?

An example of this would be when a teacher asks the whereabouts of a homework assignment and the student answers, "The dog ate it." There are two different approaches that can be taken. "Yeah, right. I've heard that one a thousand times. Can't you think of something more original?" would be the response of a teacher-centered educator focusing on the wrong issue—in this case, the morality of the student's response.

However, a statement such as "So when do you think you can get it done?" would be that of a student-centered educator who believes the possibility of a lie is irrelevant to the greater professional responsibility of helping students complete assignments. It is also a powerful message to students that they do not have to lie to educators who are primarily interested in their learning. The issue of truthfulness then becomes secondary to the students' trust that their educators are making every effort to help them succeed in school.

In the end, the Personal Self is suppressed and a **Professional Self** emerges. As this Professional Self develops, educators will experience a sense of being in a "zone of professional consciousness" that becomes the sustaining force behind every student interaction. Only when educators learn to focus on the needs of students will they lose their Personal Self in the communication and activities of an ethical professional relationship. This is the essence of a fiduciary relationship of care and trust.

31

When educators achieve this level of inspiration, talent, and commitment, professional intuition and creativity transform the student/educator relationship into an art form. Students and educators alike will sense an increased level of confidence in each other's capabilities. Educators will know they have attained this level of Professional Self when it becomes natural to respond to a contentious student by saying, "No matter what you call me or how you act, I still really care about you and will do everything I can to help you succeed in school." The outcome is a judicious style and philosophy fundamental to resolving even the most difficult of student problems.

Positive Ethical Practices

Whether consciously or subconsciously, all educators believe in some fundamental moral principles that guide them through their daily activities. The way they were raised, the books and articles read, the seminars and workshops attended, and the day by day interactions with students and colleagues have shaped in each educator a personal morality concerning professional responsibilities. As these professional values develop with experience, they should serve as constant reminders of educational strategies educators should "always" be practicing. As an example, the following are a few guiding principles I have found helpful in providing a focus for my energies and priorities. As you read these, think about those you have found successful that you would add.

1. Encourage and model an eagerness for learning and teaching. Just going through the motions is usually mirrored in the interest and behavior of students. Enthusiastic teachers who are "fired up" about learning activities, as well as the individual interests of students, are infectious.

Educators who are growing in their responsibilities by actively listening to and learning from their students, coming to their classes well-prepared, developing better methods of communication, and balancing their own activities with those of their students will continue to experience the rewards of good educational practice. These educators seldom tire of their responsibilities and almost never burn out; their flame is continually being fueled by their ongoing efforts and increased enlightenment, and, as a result, they continue to shine brighter.

2. Model a responsible professional behavior. Students should see their educators as exemplary models of professional behavior. They should exemplify such things as following through on promises, appropriate dress and language, good organization and planning, knowledge of the subject and effective teaching strategies, good work habits, and the ability to relax and enjoy others.

On the other hand, hypocrisy and inappropriate behavior combine to undermine professional integrity and have a negative effect on the efficacy of a student/educator relationship. For example, classroom teachers who drink their favorite beverage in class while not allowing students to eat or drink are in effect saying, "My personal comfort and desires are more valued in this classroom than yours." Students know immediately the difference between professional conduct and personal conduct. But educators who insist there can be two standards of personal conduct, one for them and another for students, do not understand that the real message being expressed is that educators are more valued as human beings than are students.

In the end, courtesy, dignity, and respect are community ideals educators must find ways to model if they are going to pass them on to their students.

33

3. Manifest appropriate personal behaviors. Educators must avoid expressing inappropriate personal opinions and information about their private lives to students within the school environment. For example, whether or not a teacher has ever experimented with drugs, expressions of their religious beliefs, and how they feel about certain very controversial social issues are topics that should be considered personal matters. Educators risk added discipline problems as well as loss of respect, and in some cases loss of their jobs, as the result of disclosing inappropriate information that could unduly influence the impressionable minds of students.

Instead, educators should take the initiative to share with students their hobbies, activities, and interests that show they also have a personal life outside the classroom. Knowledge that their teachers are human and that they enjoy an active and interesting personal life goes a long way in helping establish good communication between students and educators.

4. Focus efforts on motivation, encouragement, and building students' self-esteem. Encouragement from teachers communicates to students internal values such as courage, effort, and understanding, all of which enhance intrinsic feelings of self-worth. It depends not so much on concrete actions as it does on underlying attitudes. Tone of voice, inflection, and incidental inferences may change dramatically the significance of a statement or an action.

For example, the same words spoken to two different students may encourage one and discourage the other. Praising one student may lead to increased self-confidence and stimulate further effort, while another may think it was just an accident and not feel motivated toward other positive actions. Therefore, encouraging students requires constant observation of the effect.

When praise is used to manipulate students, it is a form of

external control. When it is used to give students feedback on something they have achieved, it becomes knowledge students can use to believe in themselves. Therefore, teachers would be on firmer ground by replacing praise with **recognition**. By recognizing or inquiring about accomplishments, students receive positive feedback that gives them confidence that they have done something well without the pressures of success and embarrassment sometimes brought on by praise and adulation.

For example, "So what do you think about getting 100 on your math test?" is much different from saying "Congratulations, I am so pleased you got a 100 on your math test." The question is much better in this case because it allows students to take control of their accomplishments and encourages them to express pleasure or apprehension about the perfect score. In short, encouragement is the ability to help students look better to themselves.

For students to have high self-esteem, they must feel they have value and that their individual needs and desires are considered worthy regardless of their behavior. Therefore, educators must help students learn to see themselves as significant and teach them the language that helps them separate what they **do** from who they really **are**. For example, a teacher might remind a student that "Your project received a C, not you."

In summary, it is easier to think of encouragement as not only something an educator might say to students, but just as much something students communicate to educators clarifying what **they** believe about themselves.

5. Accept the reality that students behave in ways they truly believe at that time are in their best interests. Educators must trust the fact that all student behavior is genuine and sincere before they will be able to develop the mutual respect necessary for a viable mentoring relationship. For example, telling a student "I won't help you if you're not going to try to change" is actually demeaning them by not respecting their previous attempts as authentic. In the student's mind it is a "put-down" of who they were when they tried before and who they are expected to be.

Another example would be how professionals respond when students lie. The reality of a lie exists somewhere in the student's perception of the situation. Through lying, students communicate such things as fear, lack of trust, or the power of manipulation to assure getting their own way. Regardless of the reasons, educators need to look beyond words in order to find what students are really trying to communicate. An understanding response is normally very difficult, but educators must learn to accept that lying is perceived by students as a necessary action, for what could be for **them** any number of underlying and often undeliberate reasons.

Educators do not have to agree with students' personal logic, but they must learn to respect the many ways students will view their own reality. They must "keep the faith" in the ability of students to achieve their goals and, in turn, help them meet society's expectations. Educators who show respect for students' thoughts and actions are providing that ray of hope essential for students to believe that they are truly valued.

6. Move toward learning goals and avoid performance goals. With **learning goals** (task-involved), the issue for students is to improve and learn, regardless of the mistakes or how foolish they appear. Students who set learning goals are inclined to seek challenges and persevere when they encounter problems. With **performance goals** (ego-involved), students are concerned about how they look and how they are judged by others. Students who set performance goals often experience anxiety, and are likely to avoid difficult situations and challenges and to give up when they fail.

7. Develop judicious rules and consequences that ac-

cept students as citizens. Autocratic and permissive management styles can lead to power struggles, disorganization, and alienation of students. Educators who model democratic principles seldom experience power struggles because their power is shared with students from the beginning. This pro-active approach empowers students with the principles and language of a democratic school community and provides a classroom culture that respects all students regardless of their ability, ethnicity, culture, or socio-economic class.

Only when students are allowed to exercise their human rights can they ever experience the responsibilities that flow from those freedoms. Through this language of mutual respect, tolerance, and cooperation, educators will create a democratic learning community in which students are entrusted with responsibility and the authority to be themselves.

8. Educators should feel challenged by the problems in education and be proud they are in a position to help students. Viewing problems as challenges, as opposed to avoiding them, does not come easily. However, this positive mindset is essential to the success of every professional endeavor.

To illustrate with a metaphor, imagine you have been injured severely in an automobile accident, rushed to the hospital emergency room, and are awaiting surgery. Your surgeon enters, lifts up the sheet covering your injury, winces at the sight of your condition, and exclaims: "Aaagh, this is terrible. I hate to operate on injuries like these." How would you feel about that surgeon operating on you and your chances for recovery?

On the other hand, suppose another surgeon in exactly the same circumstances lifted up the sheet and said enthusiastically: "This is going to be exciting. I haven't had an injury like this for a long time. I can't wait to get into this operation." The confidence and interest of this surgeon would probably make a difference in how you felt about the chances for successful surgery.

Would it not be the same with students with learning or behavior problems? Imagine students walking into classrooms where professional educators are excited and challenged by their problems, in contrast to classrooms where teachers openly wish those students were in someone else's classroom. When confronted by a particularly troublesome student, how many teachers would ever think to themselves: "This is going to be an exciting year. I have not had an educational challenge like this for a long time."

As much as we educators might prefer to approach problems in education with this positive attitude, this is very difficult to do day after day. But on days when educators feel challenged by student problems, they are good educators and they know it. However, on days when educators feel overcome by those same problems, they find themselves doing and saying things they know are inappropriate and unprofessional.

What is the answer? The answer lies in developing the "Professional Self" based on care and trust. As educators throw their thoughts and energies into responsible teaching and administration they tend to forget about themselves. Through study and practice comes the understanding necessary to always be acting in every students' best interests. The afterglow of mentoring students to become capable and confident individuals will linger long after the relatively short time spent helping them learn to think and act responsibly. Educators must believe in their hearts that they are better at helping students succeed than the students are at believing they are going to fail.

Disciplinary Practices to Avoid

As problems with students present themselves each day, it is sometimes difficult for educators to think of a workable approach or to keep from losing their tempers when feeling pushed to the wall. I have learned through experience, however, that there is not necessarily one "right approach" or an immediate answer to every problem that presents itself. Each situation requires that we look at it from many sides and examine numerous alternatives before taking the most appropriate action.

What has proven helpful for me is to keep in mind the things I have done in the past that were **never** successful. I hesitate to think how many times one unthinking remark or icy stare unraveled months of positive interaction and reinforcement. By the expression on the student's face, I knew I should not have done or said what I did, and I would vow afterward never to do it again.

I eventually decided that, by remembering and avoiding these unsuccessful approaches, I not only kept intact our mutual respect, but I had the time and freedom to be more creative in my search for strategies that would eventually prove successful. I have come to the conclusion that if my initial actions never make matters worse, then there is an excellent possibility that whatever actions I do take will have a better chance of helping student's recover and stay in school.

I will never forget my first "never." I began my teaching career as a music teacher in a small town in Oregon. My classroom discipline style was similar to that which I had experienced as a student. Music teachers, I reasoned, must reign supreme in both the interpretation of the music and the strict control of students. I remember being very good with sarcastic remarks to students who strayed from expected behavior. As a result, I experienced very few students who would take me on for fear of the embarrassment they would suffer.

However, there was one student who changed all of this about three months into my first year of teaching. His name was Reggie. He was a senior, a good athlete, average in achievement, and well-liked by other students. He was stubborn, outspoken, but never a problem. On the day in question he was fifteen minutes late for class. He came in and sat down in his chair, but without his instrument. Seeing this, I stopped the rehearsal and began my lecture to him on the importance of being on time. It was quite good as I elaborated a bit on the subject, thinking others would be getting the message as well. Having finished, I told him to get his horn and then we could all get back to the rehearsal.

All through this oration he had his head down, just looking at the floor. His muttered response to my demand was "I don't feel like playing today." I was incensed. I immediately began my second lecture on the importance of participation as well as laying a guilt trip as to how he was affecting the other members of the band. The whole group was silent. Reggie just looked at the floor. When I had finished my lecture he mumbled again "I don't feel like playing."

I was infuriated. Without thinking, I said the first thing that came to mind. "Reggie, If you don't play, none of us are going to play." There was silence. Reggie was still staring at the floor and the others seemed stunned by what was happening. The students really liked Reggie and were just beginning to like me as their new teacher. But I stood my ground, knowing I was right, or maybe even righteous, in my demands. After several minutes, which seemed like an hour, of this silence, the perspiration began streaming down my face. This was only one clue that what I was doing was not going to work. I was desperate.

Feeling defeated, I said the first sensible thing that came to mind. I asked the class "Does anybody have any ideas?" Karen, a clarinet player, had the answer on the tip of her tongue. She immediately said "Why don't you two guys make friends." I think I would have done anything, but that sounded like a good idea to me. I stepped down from the podium and walked back to the French horn section, held out my hand and said "Reggie, how about being friends?" He finally looked up, held out his hand, and we shook hands. At that moment the whole band began cheering. Shivers ran up my back as I walked back to the podium. I looked at Karen who was wiping away tears.

The simple expression of a handshake set in motion an enormous emotional release from the pressure I had brought upon everyone there. For the remainder of the rehearsal the band played better than they had ever played before. Even Reggie got his horn and started playing. What I learned from this experience has had a profound affect on my teaching to this day. I will always remember walking home that afternoon vowing to myself "I will never do that again."

With this brief introduction, I would like to respectfully submit my list of "nevers" and recommend that other educators consider starting their own lists based on lessons their students have taught them. As with most of life's lessons we learn well, I still wear my scars as reminders that I learned most of these the hard way—by experiencing them first hand. For this reason, I would like to dedicate the following "nevers" to all my students, past and present. I thank them sincerely for teaching me how an educator should behave.

1. Never demean students. Humiliating and embarrassing students with "put downs" always has the effect of diminishing their self-worth. Sarcasm meant to be clever, or a disparaging remark flaunting power or intellect, always hurts. Even teasing students about their appearance can be painful. Students need to live in a positive environment in which they feel they have permanent value. A positive sense of self-esteem is not something we necessarily have to give to students; more often, it is what we have to stop taking away from them.

2. Never judge or lecture students on their behavior. Instead, ask questions and listen to the student's side of the story

41

in order to learn more about the problem. We will always view problems more clearly after hearing the other side, which makes our decision better than if we had not discussed it. As the real problems surface, empower students to make decisions and allow them to choose what **they** prefer to do about it. Some will decide they are ready to make a change, while others may feel they need more time or help with the matter. This student/centered approach sends to all students a message of professional responsibility, respect for confidentiality, and a willingness to treat each as an individual.

3. Never compare students. All of us need to feel significant and accepted for who **we** are. Educators know there are many differences among students, but some fall into the trap of trying to compare these many differences with the hope it will work to motivate the unmotivated. This competitive approach almost always has the opposite effect by discouraging the desired behavior. Students simply want to be judged on their own merits and not be thrust into the shadow of others.

4. Never give students constructive criticism; always give them reflective feedback. The moment students feel they are being criticized, their thoughts are clouded by arguments defending themselves or feelings of guilt, and therefore they seldom benefit from the constructive information. Reflective feedback, on the other hand, stimulates students' thinking and discussion directed toward the heart of the matter by keeping the "teachable moment" viable. There is a considerable difference between "Let me give you some constructive criticism on your project" and "Let me give you some feedback on your project." Educators who recognize the difference have found one of the important keys to helping students become capable learners.

5. Never demand respect or think it must be earned;

learn to give it to your students. By giving it away, it is usually returned many times over. Unconditional respect, not unlike unconditional love, can only be given and received. Respect which must be earned would be conditional respect. Learning to give unconditional respect is the pathway to achieving mutual respect.

6. Never fear an apology; be grateful for a lesson learned. If we say or do something that is wrong, a sincere apology is usually gratefully accepted and a brief explanation is genuinely appreciated. This is not easy to learn, however, as we feel we are not allowed to make mistakes as educators. But eventually we learn that an apology sends a welcome message to students that they are in the presence of a sincere and honest person. Students need educators as role models as they learn the art of healing and learning from mistakes.

7. Never accuse students of not trying or ask them to try harder; always help them try again. Beginning a conversation with accusatory and judgmental statements about their previous efforts has the effect of making students want to try even less. Students experiencing problems want learning situations reinforced with positive educational strategies, not negative experiences that discourage them. Accepting students' efforts as genuine communicates a message of faith in their ability to learn. This may appear to be a subtle difference, but the student's reaction to encouragement will be one of renewed effort and interest.

8. Never ask misbehaving students "Why?"; always ask something like "What happened?" or "Would you like to tell me about it." "Why" points the finger at the person and forces students into a conversation of excuses. The other two responses focus on "what happened" or "it." Both focus on the events and are away from the person. This avoids defensiveness and leads to conversation about the problem itself. Students are far more likely to open up and talk about what happened than when they feel pressured into trying to explain reasons for what they have done. Students who are talking openly about the problem are students becoming accountable for their actions.

9. Never get into a power struggle. If a power play is developing, begin by taking your sail out of their wind and anchor yourself with a long tether. With your sail (ego) down, listening to students' wind will not blow you away; the tether (respect for their opinion) keeps you within reasoning distance. Because power struggles are no-win situations, they can only be resolved privately through an open and honest discourse that eventually leads to mutual respect. Students will know that they are valued when educators are willing to negotiate and share some of their authority. Students rarely continue to defy educators they feel are on their side and are willing to listen and work things through.

10. Never flaunt the fact that you are the educator and they are the students. In most cases students usually know when they have messed up and do not need an authority figure preaching to them about it. All they really need is a simple explanation from an educator who listens and gives them a chance to recover. When educators are sincerely making every effort to help students succeed in school, students will try very hard to help teachers succeed as educators.

11. Never become defensive or lose control of your feelings. When pride gets in the way, it has a tendency to diminish our professional qualities and leads us to do and say things we will later regret. Defensive remarks made at the height of emotional tension usually cause embarrassment for everyone.

If we begin to feel defensive, we should back off and, as calmly as possible, try to focus on a resolution using words that are devoid of emotional overtones. If we make a mistake, we need to acknowledge our error and apologize. As a result, we usually suffer very little loss of respect, and in some cases, probably gain some.

12. Never use fear and intimidation to control students. We find ourselves falling back on this approach when we run out of workable ideas. Intimidation works only in the short run, and its long range effects are unpredictable and often gave rise to other problems. Bitter feelings and sullen attitudes can develop as students became very inventive in the circuitous ways they try to get back at those who hurt them. We must learn to back away respectfully until we can think of a more student-centered approach to the problem.

13. Never punish the group for the misbehavior of one of its members. This leads to negative interdependence among the members of the classroom community. More often than not the culprit enjoys watching the group receive punishment and couldn't care less about the others. The innocent, in turn, blame the educator for punishing them unfairly. Retreat as gracefully as you can if you find yourself in this box, and find another way to handle the situation next time.

14. Never act too quickly with behavioral matters. When we would "shoot from the hip" we invariably say or do things we later regret. By coming around the problem and avoiding the "direct hit" approach, errors can more be easily corrected and the opportunity to both save face is frequently the factor that turns the corner. Unless you have had good results in the past or you are certain that what you are doing is going to work, patience, time, and plenty of discussion can be a greater ally than impulsive responses.

15. Never say "If I let you do it, I will have to let everyone else do it." Always take into consideration the individual differences among students and their varying situations. Using the excuse of what others may think in response to an educationally appropriate decision should not affect good professional practices. Rules are important for the group's welfare, but exceptions to the rules can be even more important because they recognize the legitimate differences among members of the group. The group must learn to trust that decisions regarding exceptions will be fair for all as professional judgments are made for individuals caught up in any number of diverse and often complex circumstances.

16. Never say "you will thank me someday" as a rationale for a decision that students perceive as not making sense or having any immediate purpose. Attempting to justify what we are doing by lecturing about its future benefits or disasters somewhere down the road has little effect on students. If responsible behavior has meaning here and now, we do not need to use threats to gain students' compliance. Motivational strategies and learning opportunities that address a variety of individual needs circumvent the need for lectures. Educators should want to be thanked by their students after each day, as well as some day in the future.

17. Never say "This is easy." These three little words, intended to motivate and encourage, often become a monkey on the backs of students who feel insecure about their abilities. Even those who feel secure need feedback that what they are doing is something more than "easy." We should always be aware that all students do not share our interests nor have our abilities and try to understand the task more from a student's viewpoint than our own. Being interested in their difficulties and feelings of success has an immediate effect of bolstering their confidence and feelings of self-worth.

18. Never think that being consistent means treating all students alike. Consistency in education is providing the professional specialization and skills needed to help each student believe success is possible. Students know they have different personalities and abilities that require various educational strategies in order to meet their many needs and goals. They deeply respect educators who understand that one style of teaching or discipline should not necessarily be applied to everyone. Being consistent, therefore, means meeting each student's needs. We must listen to and observe all of our students carefully as we learn to appreciate and judiciously manage their individual differences.

Student Ethics

As students learn more about ethics and understand the important role they play in our society, teachers could help them compose their own "Ethics of Appropriate Behavior." During class meetings students could prepare a list of behavioral goals and principles to guide them in matters of school and community living. Topics such as honesty, promptness, personal hygiene, initiative, cooperation, mutual respect, accountability, concern for the welfare of others, and ways they can help others in the class learn and feel better about themselves would be only a few examples.

Using an interactive approach, Margaret Abbott's fourth grade class in West Linn, Oregon, developed the following statement of ethics. When finished, they posted the statement near their previously-developed classroom rules (see description of those rules in Chapter 4, page 94) to show how the two are interrelated and equally important. The statement of ethics reads:

1. We would like to be treated with respect.
2. We would like others to be considerate of our feelings.
3. When papers are displayed, we would like to have all class members' papers displayed, not just a few.
4. We would like to be treated equally, but not the same.
5. We want to be able to trust our teacher to give matching consequences when a rule is broken, and not embarrass us.
6. We would like the people in the class to be responsible for themselves.
7. We would like the people in the class to be considerate of our ideas and opinions.
8. When we disagree with someone, we can be polite and not explode.
9. We want people to help people when they need it, but not give the answers. (No help on tests.)

Other ideas for ethical discourse could include how students would behave toward others learning from their mistakes, how they themselves should respond to and learn from the consequences of their actions, and how to separate their misbehavior from their value as a human being. In addition, asking for student opinions regarding the teacher's handling of classroom problems would be a worthwhile activity for educators who are ready to share their classroom responsibilities and authority.

When the list is ready, with space for additions, it could be posted near the class rules so all may see it. In this way, everyone will be able to read and reread it as a constant reminder of how the students themselves have decided they want to behave towards others as well as the way they want others to treat them.

In summary, classroom discussions of ethical principles allow students to elaborate on the meaning and importance of ethics in their daily interactions with others. A free and open expression of attitudes between students and their teachers not only sets out mutually shared principles but also creates an excellent model for moral development.

Professional Statement of Ethics

Educators' professional ethics are usually passed along through their daily interactions with students. Although the course syllabus reflects closely the educational philosophy and standards of the teacher, rarely does one see in writing an educator's statement of ethics. Students, seeing a statement of ethics drafted by their teacher and posted for all to view, witness a refreshing message of openness and commitment by an educator secure in his or her Professional Self.

The statement of ethics could include ideas taken from "Positive Ethical Practices" concerning professional priorities and behavior. Another source would be from the list of "nevers" in the section "Disciplinary Practices to Avoid." By drawing on material from this chapter on ethics and adding statements based on personal experiences, educators should have a good start on a statement of professional conscience reflecting a commitment to helping every student succeed.

A statement of professional ethics also provides an excellent vehicle for class discussion as educators look for ways to make known their philosophy of teaching and learning. By allowing students an opportunity to react and express their opinions, teachers are modeling a risk-taking activity as they create an open forum management style. Leaving room on the Statement of Ethics for additions shows it is a dynamic expression of conscience. This open-ended document illustrates that experience is a good teacher, while also communicating to others that courage to share authority and personal growth are clearly linked.

In summary, the ethics of any profession are at best fragile and difficult to manage when put into practice. Initially, educators must exhibit a general concern for ethical behavior—given the fact that morality is, generally speaking, a matter of personal character. For ethics to be viable, there must be a continuing, on-going moral and ethical inquiry. When educators wear well the mantle of their responsibility, biases and personalities take a secondary status to the needs students have to be guided.

To our students we appear larger than life and, therefore, must personify a model worthy of imitation. It is imperative that we keep alive our students' belief that we are acting in their best interests through a strong and viable student/educator relationship of trust and care. In the final analysis, a teacher's classroom is a student's world.

CHAPTER 3:
A CONSTITUTIONAL PERSPECTIVE FOR SCHOOL RULES

I t is not uncommon to hear educators express frustration over the plethora of legal issues they are required to understand and implement. This feeling of futility is often attributed to a national shift from the school's protectiveness of *"in loco parentis,"* a legal phrase meaning the school stands in the place of a parent, to the realization that students "no longer shed their constitutional rights at the school house gate." It may be frustrating for many of us to make the change from a parental approach of disciplining students to learning about their constitutional rights and how those rights apply to the school setting. In other words, our public schools and classrooms have become, in fact, microcosms of the United States of America.

In order to create a school culture where students' human rights are respected, students and educators will need to learn a new language—the language of civility. Because every culture is grounded in its language, the first step is to learn something about our nation's democratic principles and how they can be integrated into the school environment.

This point is brought home when students confront educators

51

with a statement like "You can't do that to me, I've got my rights." Asked to explain what they mean by their rights, most respond by saying something like "I don't know, but I've got my rights." Although many students and parents talk about having rights, few really understand the actual meaning.

The purpose of Chapter 3 is to help educators learn to speak and act with self-assurance on the subject of student rights. It provides a brief review of the constitutional law applicable to public education. Students and educators alike will find that the principles of democracy work well as a foundation for building learning communities. One of the distinguishing characteristics of a democratic educational environment is that it helps students understand and appreciate society's diversity. In short, this chapter provides the legal basis of a judicious model for student discipline.

⚖️

The Bill of Rights

Students will graduate into a system of constitutional government that not only bestows specific freedoms on each individual but also provides for the needs, interests, and welfare of the majority. Individual rights are not guaranteed, but neither are they easily denied by the majority. Growing up in America, most of us learned that democracy is a system of government in which the majority rules. We used this to settle playground arguments by voting on what game to play or seeking a consensus on the rules. When watching and listening to children play today, we realize this approach to even the most unstructured activities has not changed.

Students continue to learn the concept of "the majority rules," but seldom in their upbringing do they learn about individual rights. It is important, therefore, that students understand that in our nation's constitutional democracy, human rights are equally important as the needs and interests of the majority. How our society judiciously balances individual rights with the welfare of the majority is how we all live productively and peaceably together in America.

It all begins with the Bill of Rights, the first ten amendments to the United States Constitution, which were written to protect three basic human values: **freedom, justice,** and **equality**. Although the Constitution and Bill of Rights have been further amended over the years, and now contain a total of twenty-six amendments, such changes have simply fleshed out the meaning of these human rights principles. Any discussion with students about their "rights," therefore, would flow from one of these three concepts. These three American values have their antecedents in the Constitution and are fundamental to understanding the meaning of human rights.

The controversy over the question of how, when, and where to limit individual **freedoms** is a never-ending question our society constantly seeks to balance. Living in a free society, however, does not mean we have license to do as we please. It means we have freedom to think and act on behalf of our own self-interests, but only as balanced with the welfare needs of other members of the larger community. For younger students freedom means **"choices."** Students know when they are empowered to make decisions in contrast to when they are obeying directives made by others. The difficulty, of course, always lies in devising a precise formula to indicate when freedom has exceeded rightful bounds.

Justice is concerned primarily with due process and deals with basic governmental fairness. Those in America enjoy the substantive right to be governed by fair and reasonable laws. Justice also provides for the procedural right of adequate notice, a fair hearing, and the right to appeal laws and decisions that take away life, liberty, and property. Most students at an early age develop a sense of **"fairness"** when it concerns rules and consequences. They also recognize and appreciate those who take the time to **"hear their opinion"** on matters important to them. The safeguards provided by our nation's justice system are well-conceived, but as with most systems in our culture, the forces of economics, politics, and the "human factor" cause it occasionally to fail; it simply is not equal to the task in every case.

Finally, **equality** presents us with the problem of distributing burdens and benefits. The proposition that "all people are created equal" has never meant that we all possess the same abilities, interests, or talents. Although all students may not be achieving the same or performing at the same level in their public school, it is the **opportunity** to succeed in public education that is the constitutional right which must be "equal to all." In other words, equality does not mean treating all students equally, but instead treating them in the many different ways necessary to meet their diverse needs in order that they are able to succeed in school. When students feel they have a **"chance for success"** in school then educators are meeting both the letter and spirit of this basic human right.

The source of these three basic values springs from the First, Fourth, and Fourteenth Amendments. Although other amendments and legislative laws are occasionally applied to student learning and behavior issues, students and educators knowledgeable about three key amendments to the Constitution have a solid foundation when "talking about student rights." Let's examine them more closely.

The First Amendment

Congress shall make no law respecting an establishment

*of religion or prohibiting the free exercise thereof; or
abridging the freedom of speech or of the press; or of the
people peaceably to assemble, and to petition the government for a redress of grievances.*

The First Amendment was designed to insure certain basic
personal freedoms that, until the late 1960s, were seldom applied
to students in American public schools. However, in recent years
numerous judicial decisions related to matters concerning free
speech have been litigated. Length of boys' hair, dress and
appearance, and slogans on clothing are only a few examples.
Freedom of the **press** has also generated considerable litigation
concerning student rights to publish and distribute material on
school premises.

The two clauses in the First Amendment which relate to
religion continue to have considerable impact on public educational programs. Of all the amendments in the Bill of Rights,
those related to church-state relationships have been the most
difficult to litigate and apply to our school system. The court's
adjudication of this provision has left educators with considerable
latitude for their own interpretations. As a result, a certain
amount of subtle and unknowing discrimination remains in
many public schools today. The right of students to **assemble
peaceably** also remains a controversial issue on school cam-
puses, especially as students become more knowledgeable of
their civil rights.

The Fourth Amendment

*The right of the people to be secure in their persons,
houses, papers, and effects, against unreasonable searches
and seizures, shall not be violated, and no warrants shall
issue, but upon probable cause, supported by oath or*

affirmation, and particularly describing the place to be searched, and the persons or things to be seized.

This amendment presents an issue of practical importance to all educators who take property from students. Student expectancy of privacy can range from the posting of names for disciplinary reasons to searches of lockers, purses, pockets, or student vehicles in the parking lot. Although most educators do not consider themselves to have the same societal charge as that of law enforcement officers, effective school management requires them to use similar guidelines when taking property from students.

The Fourteenth Amendment

*All persons born or naturalized in the United States, and subject to the jurisdiction thereof, are citizens of the United States and of the State wherein they reside. No State shall make or enforce any law which shall abridge the privileges or immunities of citizens of the United States; **nor shall any State deprive any person of life, liberty, or property without due process of law; nor deny to any person the equal protection of the laws.***

The last two clauses of the Fourteenth Amendment have had significant impact on public education. The first of these, known as the **"due process clause,"** provides the legal basis for reasonable rules and a fair process for balancing student rights. The last clause, known as the **"equal protection clause,"** serves as the constitutional foundation for prohibiting all forms of discrimination. This clause is broadly interpreted in cases dealing with all forms of discrimination, including discrimination based on gender, race, national origin, disabilities, marital status, age, and religion, and assures an equal educational opportunity for all students.

The Fourteenth Amendment acts as the fulcrum for our somewhat fragile constitutional form of government. Educators who understand and are able to apply the concepts of due process are usually perceived as possessing a sense of justice and equality when resolving student conflicts. Because of its importance, the next several pages have been devoted to the meaning of due process.

Due Process

....nor shall any State deprive any person of life, liberty or property, without due process of law;....

Picture the blindfolded woman symbolizing justice that adorns the thresholds of our country's courthouses. Standing strong and confident, her outstretched arm is holding the familiar scales of justice. Imagine one scale heaped to the brim with the majority of the boys and girls in your school. On the other side of the scale, picture the one lone student standing with books and lunch sack in hand, gazing apprehensively at all the other students amassed on the opposite side. This image symbolizes the balancing of separate interests and is the essence of "due process" as applied to public schools.

In its simplest terms, due process is a legal effort to balance the welfare of the majority with the countless needs and desires of individuals in our culturally rich and diverse society. Only when the state is able to show a compelling reason why public welfare should weigh more than individual rights, will the court's scale of justice swing toward the interests of the majority. Conversely, if the government cannot demonstrate a compelling state interest, then the rights of a single student will weigh more heavily than all who crowd the other side of the scale.

Although written succinctly, the due process clause represents two hundred years of legislation and court decisions clarifying and interpreting its meaning. To fully understand and appreciate the complexity of this constitutional concept, let's break it down and examine the due process concept a few words at a time.

"...**nor shall any State**" means that in order to have a right to due process there must be state action. When applied to education, only students in **public** schools enjoy due process rights; their counterparts in our nation's private institutions do not have similar constitutional rights. The legal rights of students in the private sector are expressly set out in the contract between parents or guardians and the corporation that administers the school. Speaking in legal terms, students dismissed from private schools would therefore be considered guilty of breaching their part of the contract between their parents and the private institution. The logic of the law implies that students who disobey or are not satisfied with the rules of a private school are admittedly free to choose another. On the other hand, public funding by the state creates the state action necessary for students' rights to due process in public schools.

"...**deprive any person**" means withholding these constitutional rights from any person within the jurisdiction of the United States. The law has been extended to include non-citizens as well as those who are in the United States illegally. This is not to say they have a right to live here, but they do have the right to due process while living here, including the right to legal proceedings that may lead to their deportation. "Any person" is broadly interpreted by the courts and today includes all students in our public schools.

"...**of life, liberty, or property**" defines those rights that may be deprived through due process by governmental action. It is interesting to note that the framers of our Constitution used just three words to protect our past, present, future, and even death at the hands of the government. For example, the word "**property**" includes everything a person legally owns and has acquired up to the present. It covers tangible properties such as real estate, personal property, and money, as well as intangibles such as contracts of employment, eligibility and entitlement to welfare payments, as well as the property rights of students to attend public schools.

The second word, "**liberty**," begins with the present and embodies all future acquisitions and aspirations:

> ...it denotes not merely freedom from bodily restraint but also the right of the individual to contract, to engage in any of the common occupations of life, to acquire useful knowledge, to marry, establish a home and bring up students, to worship God according to the dictates of his own conscience, and generally to enjoy those privileges long recognized...as essential to the orderly pursuit of happiness by free men. (*Meyer v. Nebraska*, 262 US 390, 399 [1923])

Educators committed to student success and who sincerely care about students' future opportunities exemplify the importance of liberty within the meaning and spirit of the Constitution.

Finally, the word "**life**" refers to the loss of personal life at the hands of the government, such as the execution of a criminal.

"...**without due process of law**" means the process due persons being deprived their life, liberty, or property by governmental authority. Clarifying its application to everyday situations, court decisions have separated "due process" into two distinct aspects: **substantive** and **procedural**.

"Substantive due process" pertains to the legislation, the rule, or the law itself. It means a basic fairness and legality in the substance of the decision. If the state attempted to deprive a person of life, liberty, or property, substantive due process would require a valid objective and means that are reasonably calculated to achieve the objective. The rule or law should:

1. have some rational need for its adoption,
2. be as good in meeting the need as any alternative that reasonable people would have developed,
3. be supported by relevant and substantial evidence and findings of fact.

In other words, substantive due process implies that laws and decisions must be legal before our government can deprive persons of their life, liberty, or property. For example, a class at school that is limited to only girls or only boys would violate students' substantive due process rights because discriminating on the basis of gender violates the equal protection clause of the Fourteenth Amendment. When any class is offered in a public school, both sexes have a **property** right to that education; further, both can show that being barred from the class could also affect their **liberty** by limiting their future opportunities. Whenever someone questions a rule or seeks clarification of a decision, they are exercising their substantive due process rights.

"Procedural due process" relates to the decision-making process used when determining whether a rule or law has been violated. Basic fairness in adjudication is required and has been interpreted by the courts to contain the following:

1. Adequate notice,
2. A fair and impartial hearing,
3. The right to appeal the decision.

Adequate notice includes such procedures as charges, evidence to be used against the person charged, a reasonable amount of time to prepare a defense, the time and place of the hearing, and adequacy of form (oral and written). **A fair and impartial hearing** encompasses elements such as a meaningful opportunity to be heard, to state a position, and to present witnesses. It also may include the right to counsel, presentation and cross-examination of witnesses, and review of written reports in advance of the hearing. **The right of appeal** is not only applicable to our state and federal court system, but is an integral part of our governmental structure as students exhaust their administrative remedies by appealing rules and decisions made by school personnel.

Every rule or decision made in a public institution is subject to review by another person, board, or court. With few exceptions, the **Due Process Clause** allows all administrative decisions, as well as the rule in question, to be appealed through the institution's administrative structure. From the institution, the decision or rule may be appealed to a higher state or federal administrative agency and then to an appropriate court.

For example, an educator who says to an inquiring student "There is nothing you can do about it—this is a non-appealable decision" is bluffing. All rules and decisions in public education are appealable. Because of this, many educators are reluctant to inform students they have this right of appeal because they know it is possible for their administrative decision or rule to some day reach as far as the United States Supreme Court.

Due process, as is the case with many legal concepts, resists a simple dictionary definition and tends to be a dynamic rather than a static concept.

Rights in School

Until 1969, court decisions historically supported the concept of *in loco parentis*, which granted to educators the same legal authority over students as that of parents. In the absence of "state action" implicit in the Fourteenth Amendment, students who live with parents enjoy no constitutional rights. For example, parents searching their child's bedroom without a search warrant would not violate his or her Fourth Amendment rights from unreasonable search and seizure, or a daughter or son denied the keys to the family car for the evening would have no Fourteenth Amendment right to appeal their parents' decision. The legal precedent of *in loco parentis* allowed public schools the same ultimate authority, provided their rules were not unreasonable, capricious, arbitrary, malicious, or made in bad faith.

There is legislation, however, that protects children from their parents. State child-abuse laws and federal child-labor legislation are two examples of society's means of safeguarding children from abusive parental acts. Early court decisions applied this "abuse test" to protect students in public schools, but unless educators were clearly abusive, courts would not intercede. The courts presumed professional educators were more knowledgeable about matters of student development and discipline than were judges and juries. Parents' knowledge that they carried the burden of proof and their fear of retaliatory acts against their children prevented most from seeking redress in court. In situations where parents did sue for relief school districts generally prevailed.

Today the situation is much different. Courts rarely use the concept of *in loco parentis* when writing opinions on student disciplinary issues. This concept has been replaced by language that addresses the constitutional rights and responsibilities of students. Although there have been prior questions considered, the United States Supreme Court in *Tinker v. Des Moines Independent School District*, 393 U.S. 503, for the first time held that students in public schools have constitutional rights in the area of student discipline. This case, cited ritualistically by school authorities as well as student plaintiffs, establishes general guidelines applicable to many school situations.

The Tinker case involved high school students suspended by their principal for wearing black arm bands to school in protest to the United States' involvement in Vietnam. The students won the right to express their political beliefs when the court stated for the first time:

> ...First Amendment rights, applied in light of the special characteristics of the school environment, are available to teachers and students. It can hardly be argued that either students or teachers shed their constitutional rights to freedom of speech or expression at the schoolhouse gate...

It is apparent that times have changed from the days when school rules were arbitrary and resembled those used in most families. Today, the rules school authorities use must take into consideration the constitutional rights of students.

If, in fact, students do not shed their constitutional rights at the schoolhouse gate, then a graphic illustration of student rights might be to imagine students dressing each morning in attire selected from their wardrobe of liberties. By the time they have donned their mail of **"freedom,"** buckled on a sword of **"justice,"** and grasped the shield of **"equality,"** they might be reminiscent of knights of King Arthur's Round Table, clad in full battle dress as they walk the hallways of our public schools.

This may be seen as a formidable image, and in many cases very intimidating to educators who come face to face with student discipline problems every day. To complicate matters, frustrated educators are frequently heard to say "The students seem to have more rights than I have."

This, in fact, happens to be true. Educators have no constitutional rights in the student/educator relationship. Only students have rights in that relationship; educators have responsibilities. Because our civil rights only protect us from government action, educators are the government in student/educator interactions. As a result, public school educators have the legal responsibility of respecting and ensuring student rights, but they do not enjoy the same rights from their students.

The constitutional rights public educators do enjoy, however, are those which flow between them and their government, which happens to be their supervising administrators and the school board. In other words, their rights come down to them from the employer/employee relationship, not up to them from the student/educator relationship. As employees, for example, teachers have a right to leave school to celebrate their religious holidays, but they cannot freely exercise their religious beliefs in their classrooms. As a result, educators should think in terms of their students as having "rights" and of themselves as having legal and professional "responsibilities" to ensure those student rights.

We are now at the core, the very heart of the question facing disciplinary issues in public schools today. **Is there a way to establish and maintain an effective learning environment in our schools, while at the same time respecting student rights of freedom, justice, and equality?**

Compelling State Interests

As foreboding as respecting students' constitutional rights appear at first blush, there is another very important side to the scale of justice. There are, in fact, four time-tested public interest arguments crafted in the courts and construed for the precise purpose of limiting constitutionally protected freedoms. These arguments are as well-grounded in legal principle and history as the line of reasoning that allows for individual rights.

Authority for denying persons their civil rights comes from Article I, Section 8, of the Constitution, which reads in part "...The Congress shall have Power to...provide for the common Defense and general Welfare of the United States." This "**general welfare clause**" acts as the legal foundation for legislative bodies to represent the needs and interests of the majority.

This legal concept is commonly referred to as **compelling state interests,** and simply means that in some cases the welfare and interests of the majority are more compelling than those of an individual—any individual. This welfare principle, used in conjunction with our government's responsibility, gives educators all the legal authority they need to create and carry out fair and equitable school rules.

The legality of a school rule is generally presumed, and the burden of proof to change it rests with the complaining student. On the other hand, if a rule actually infringes on a fundamental constitutional right, the burden of proof then shifts to school officials to demonstrate a compelling state need. For example, the need to maintain a learning environment free from serious disruption would be a compelling state interest allowing schools to prohibit excessive noise during class or fighting on the playground or other similar conduct detrimental to the school's interest. The closer laws come to encroaching on student substantive rights, the greater the need for justification and clarification by school authorities.

With the understanding that educators must have a compelling state interest in order to sustain their rules and decisions, this begs the question: **What are these compelling state interests?**

For years, our nation's courts have been using four basic arguments in an effort to sustain the balance between the individual and the state's interest in our public schools. These compelling state interests are as follows:

1. Property loss or damage,
2. Legitimate educational purpose,
3. Threat to health and safety,
4. Serious disruption of the educational process.

In other words, school rules and decisions based on these four compelling state interest arguments will, in all probability, withstand the test of today's court rulings despite the fact that they deny students their individual rights. Educators not only have a legal authority to deny student constitutional rights, but it is their professional responsibility to prohibit student behaviors when their exercise of those rights seriously affects the welfare of the school. Let's examine each of the four interests and apply them to the school setting.

Property Loss or Damage

"Wear appropriate shoes on the gym floor."
"Respect the property of others."
"Return the athletic equipment after you play with it."

Care of property is usually an easy concept for students to understand and few argue their right to damage school facilities or take the property of others. However, years of public schooling provides students many opportunities to remove or perhaps damage state-owned property. Taxpayers, therefore, rely heavily on the sound judgment of educators to oversee the care and maintenance of public property entrusted to them. Further, parents also depend on school personnel to assist in protecting their student's property within the jurisdiction of school authority. Rules must be explicit and reasonably related to the loss or damage intended to be prevented in order to insure adequate notice.

Legitimate Educational Purpose

> *"It is compulsory for all school-age students to attend school."*
> *"Bring your school supplies and books to class."*
> *"Our lesson today is the correct use of pronouns."*

Every public body has the legal authority to promulgate rules to carry out its legislative purpose. For public schools, this means making educational rules and consequences for the purpose of helping students succeed in school. Educators are considered experts in matters of academic decisions that include course content, rigor, and student achievement. Plagiarism, classroom and homework assignments, grading practices, special or advanced placement, and all other decisions and procedures that are designed to enhance students' learning are illustrations of the scope of this compelling state interest. Courts are reluctant to second-guess educational decisions based on sound professional judgment. However, some cases involving conflicts with family values will tip the scales in favor of individual rights, such as the example of students being excused from classes teaching the Theory of Evolution.

Generally speaking, all policies and decisions having a tenable educational motive related to appropriate school objectives come within the intent of this standard. But as students obtain jobs in the private sector, legitimate educational purpose then changes to legitimate employer purpose. Or when dealing with other governmental agencies such as law enforcement, rules and decisions would be based on legitimate police purposes. When educators make professional decisions, it may appear to students as rather arbitrary, but certainly no less so than an employer who arbitrarily requires a uniform because it is "good for business." If students trust that their educators are making decisions in their best interests, few will question their legitimate educational purpose.

Threat to Health and Safety

> *"Move carefully in the halls."*
> *"Be healthy and safe toward others."*
> *"Language must be appropriate for the school environment."*

A fundamental purpose of government is to protect the health and welfare of its citizens. This not only includes their physical health, but their psychological and emotional health as well. The compelling need to protect children in their custody is especially applicable to educators who govern America's public schools. Courts consistently sustain rules and decisions designed to maintain the health and safety of the majority and are quick to deny individual freedoms that threaten others.

The importance of health and safety rules is apparent in school situations that expose students to such dangers as playgrounds, shops, science labs, physical education, and sports. Although students may complain about rules that prohibit rough play and fighting, or require the use of protective equipment, school authorities must take steps to insure their own health and safety and that of others. If student rights are being balanced with a potential student injury, it is far better for educators to err on the side of health and safety. In addition, the emotional health of many students is often violated by the use of bigoted statements, harrassing behavior, and vulgar expressions as they rightfully pursue a healthy and safe education. Students will receive lifetime benefits from health and safety rules that are designed with society's welfare in mind. To be effective, these rules should be all inclusive, conspicuous, and rigorously enforced.

Serious Disruption of the Educational Process

"Tardy students should come quietly into the classroom."
"Keep your hands and feet to yourself."
"Consider others when talking in class."

The establishment and enforcement of rules that foster a proper educational environment are necessary to the successful operation of every school. School officials have both the legal authority and the professional responsibility to deny student rights that seriously disrupt student activities. At first glance, "serious disruption" may appear to be uncomplicated and easily defined. However, consideration must be given to three very important questions before a judicious decision should be rendered. Because of their importance, let's examine these questions.

What is serious? The language of today's courts stipulates that in order to deny students their rights "the disruption must materially and/or substantially interfere with the requirements of appropriate discipline in the operation of the public schools." Each situation must be decided on its own merits and may vary from one classroom to another in the same building. For example, the acceptable hubbub of one class could or could not be a serious disruption in another class, depending on differences in teaching strategies or educational content.

The Supreme Court in the *Tinker* case considered closely whether students wearing black armbands to school did or did not seriously disrupt the student body. The Court stated:

> Only a few of the 18,000 students in the school system wore the black armbands. Only five students were suspended for wearing them. There is no indication that the work of the school or any class was disrupted. Outside the classrooms, a few students made hostile remarks to the students wearing armbands, but there were no threats or acts of violence on school premises. In order for the State in the person of school officials to justify prohibition of a particular expression of opinion, it must be able to show that its action was caused by something more than a mere desire to avoid the discomfort and unpleasantness that always accompany an unpopular viewpoint.

It is important to note the last sentence of the court's ruling, because it gives us some sense of "what is serious." Apparently "serious" means more than just actions and expressions that are unpleasant or make others feel uncomfortable. If the act or expression is a serious disruption, student rights will give way to society's expectations. If it is not serious, educators should make every effort to help an inconvenienced or annoyed majority understand the value of and reasons for individual rights. In order for democracy to work, civil rights and tolerance must be understood and practiced together.

Must the serious disruption have already occurred, or is the threat of a serious disruption enough to sustain the rule or decision? Again, we turn to the words of the Tinker decision for guidance:

> ...in our system, undifferentiated fear or apprehension of disturbance is not enough to overcome the right to freedom of expression. Any departure from absolute regimentation may cause trouble. Any variation from the majority's opinion may inspire

70

fear. Any word spoken, in class, in the lunchroom or on the campus, that deviates from the views of another person, may start an argument or cause a disturbance. But our Constitution says we must take this risk; and our history says that it is this sort of hazardous freedom—this kind of openness—that is the basis of our national strength and of the independence and vigor of Americans who grow up and live in the relatively permissive, often disputatious society.

Often rules and decisions are based on the fear that something may occur when, in fact, it may never have happened and is not likely to happen. This, of course, varies greatly from one situation to another and could make congruous decisions difficult. The fact that the school board bears the burden of proof as to whether or not the wearing of armbands "...might reasonably have led school authorities to forecast substantial disruption..." also compounds the issue. To what extent should educators be permitted to adopt preventive rules and when is it required to wait "until the horse is stolen before locking the barn door?"

This is a most difficult question, yet one that educators must resolve daily. Good educators concerned about student rights will seek out the best advice available, balance this knowledge in the context of both their duty to the state and to individual rights, and resolve it with a "best effort" decision. Although possibly disgruntled by the decision, those affected will appreciate the thoughtful consideration and professional demeanor exhibited by the process.

For whom should the rule be intended, the individual who is exercising constitutional rights or the majority who are disquieted by the individual's exercise of those rights? The Tinker decision helps clarify the issue.

Students in school as well as out of school are "persons" under our Constitution. They are possessed of fundamental rights

71

which the State must respect, just as they themselves must respect their obligations to the State. Judge Gewin, speaking for the Fifth Circuit, said that school officials cannot suppress, expressions of feelings with which they do not wish to contend.

Educators, for example, often will ban the wearing of hats in school because of disruptions caused when other students take the hats and throw them about the classroom. Although it may be administratively more convenient to threaten suspension of a few hat-wearing students, denying individual expression because of disruptions brought on by others is inherently unfair. Rather, educators today must assume a leadership role for safeguarding individual student rights by designing rules and strategies to help students understand the civilized nature of tolerance and their responsibility for living with the many differences expressed by other members of the school community.

However, this is not easily accomplished. Balancing the obligation to provide for the liberties of a single student with the pressures brought about by the clamor of the majority can add up to a lot of heat in the new schoolhouse kitchen. As a result, knowledge and practice of *Judicious Discipline* is pivotal to the success of responding rationally and consistently to inquiring students and parents.

Prior to the 1970s, when educators were asked by students to explain the reason for a rule, the response could have been something like "Because I am your teacher and this is the way we do it here" or "You will have to learn to follow rules some day so you might as well learn to follow mine." The response was usually fairly arbitrary and commonly known as having rules for rules' sake. Common thinking held that students needed to learn obedience and obedient students were responsible students.

A student today, however, would hear a different response to the same question. It might sound something like "Let me tell you my compelling state interest for the rule." Although the rule may be the same in both situations, the language and legal rationale has changed substantially in order to respect student rights.

But in its final analysis, **students must understand that their rights do not allow them to do as they please**. Student rights are properly denied when their actions infringe on the property and well-being of others.

Notes:

CHAPTER 4:
THE DEMOCRATIC SCHOOL COMMUNITY

E ducators who want to create a democratic environment must approach rules and consequences as a way of building community and keeping students in school, rather than using them as a means for pushing students out. This judicious mindset would view rules as **guidelines** as opposed to restrictions and use consequences for **learning** and **restitutional** purposes instead of for punishing students. In short, *Judicious Discipline* was developed as a foundation for educators who are using strategies designed to encourage students to stay in school.

The problem lies in one of our educational system's more glaring contradictions—the autocratic schools we use for teaching students to be responsible citizens in a democratic society. Ironically, the first experience most students have with government is when their state's compulsory education laws require them to attend school. They are forced into a system of rules and decisions not unlike the authority they encounter at home, an authority that rewards obedience, punishes offenders, and needs no justification other than "I am the authority here."

If the management system in our public schools parallels the autocratic environment of most American homes, it follows that parents and educators may be preparing graduates who are unable to understand or function well in a participatory society. It is no surprise that parents occasionally ask their children "When are you going to grow up and begin thinking for yourself?" In the long run, the benefits of enabling students to think and act as responsible citizens far outweigh the disciplinary expediency of teaching blind obedience.

But because most educators fear losing control over their students, they are reluctant to move away from autocratic methods. It is very important, therefore, that students and educators both understand from the beginning that **a democratic classroom does not mean there is a permissive environment or that every decision is decided by a majority vote**. But unlike an autocratic environment, it does begin by recognizing and establishing the principles of human rights leading to the counterbalancing principles of the compelling needs of the state. The principles of a democracy offer considerable structure for government to prescribe proper civil behavior and place a great deal of authority in the hands of governmental officials.

When democratic principles are applied to a classroom, teachers would be analogous to governmental officials and would have the same authority to enforce rules and resolve disputes among classroom members. In every democracy, there is a critical need for good leadership in order to keep its principles strong and viable. The same is true of educators in a democratic school community. How much more effective our schools could be if we would teach the rationale for society's boundaries and the intrinsic value of responsible behavior. Until students are allowed to have some control over their actions and begin to feel an ownership in their learning community, their desire to function responsibly will always be at risk.

The Perspective in Practice

Educators must adopt a democratic way of thinking if they are going to respect their students as citizens. This democratic mindset may be illustrated by using as an example a rule common to many classrooms—"No chewing gum." This rule is widely enforced in order to keep gum from under desks and seats, out of hair and/or textbooks, from being popped or chewed noisily, as well as prevent the litter of gum wrappers.

Envision, if you will, a new student entering your classroom at mid-semester, wearing a three-piece suit, hand-made Italian shoes, carrying a briefcase and a lap top computer, and chewing the biggest wad of gum you have ever seen. His admit slip indicates he is the sole heir of a family who are the principal shareholders in a very large chewing gum corporation. Inquiring about the gum in his mouth, you are told that he is simply carrying on a family tradition symbolic of their commitment to the idea that gum can be chewed properly and is acceptable in a social setting. In other words, in this scenario his chewing gum is a statement of personal belief and an expression of family values based on his First Amendment right of free speech.

Although the example exaggerates to emphasize a point, there may be a rational basis for the student's argument. Promulgating rules in public schools today necessitates bringing the rule within the meaning of one of the state's four compelling interests. If none of the four would be applicable, it would be unconstitutional to deny his right to chew gum. Therefore, if educators are going to move away from autocratic classrooms and respect students as citizens, they must learn to apply the state's rationale. With this in mind, let's look at how this scenario might play out.

Property damage is the rationale commonly used to restrict gum chewing in class. However, this reasoning may break down if it can be established that damage does not occur when students chew gum, but only when gum is out of their mouths. Perhaps the rule banning gum necessitates a place to hide it and, therefore, the rule against chewing gum is the major cause of damage. A better rule to protect property might be a rule prohibiting gum from being out of students' mouths unless wrapped in paper.

Legitimate educational purpose would not be congruous unless one wanted to legislate the morality of chewing gum. Legislating morality is always controversial because it begs the question of "whose morality." Teaching students the proper use of gum, however, would be more appropriate to educational purpose. Therefore, the only values educators can legislate are those values of civility which come within the meaning of the four compelling state interests.

Health and safety would be a good reason to teach the health advantages to sugarless gum. Students' safety would certainly be a compelling reason to enforce a rule against gum chewing during physical activities in order to prevent a student from choking. Specific rules against popping and chewing loudly should be enough to prevent a **serious disruption of the educational process**.

Although this scenario may appear contrived, it is an example of how educators can begin to look differently at rules traditionally used to teach students obedience. Purposeless rules such as "No gum" and "No hats," strictly enforced, simply destroy educational credibility and leave suspect all other rules and subsequent decisions.

The time and effort spent on enforcement alone pushes

students and educators away from the important aspects of learning. Rules that respect students' rights make sense and have a way of empowering everyone.

The advantage of formulating school rules founded on our nation's principles of human rights is that they are not easily interpreted by students as being arbitrary or capricious. And more importantly, educators are not personally identified with the rules. When personal biases are used as the basis for rules and decisions, educators are more likely to interpret rule violations as personal affronts against themselves. As a result, educators often become defensive. When this happens, there is an escalation of personality conflicts that have no relevance to the validity of the rule or the consequences that may follow.

A shared knowledge of constitutional principles and societal welfare interests allows objectivity. The educator's role is analogous to a third party whose responsibility it is to shepherd the relationship between students and society's reasonable expectations.

The fruits of this labor are clearly felt when calmly responding to a quarrelsome student: "Let's look at our school's rules another way. Did you know they are based on the same principles and rationale under which you live when you're not in school." Two hundred plus years of integrated wisdom and legal authority properly presented and discussed can work wonders for educators seeking to bring about equanimity in their classrooms.

An Educational Approach

All too often, educators find themselves inventing an endless parade of rules, hoping to create the illusion of being in control. Many are convinced that confronting students with a "line in the dirt" and the fear of being punished for crossing it is the way to force compliance with school rules.

The problem with this thinking, however, is once an educator's line is crossed the illusion of being in control begins to unravel. When this happens, the "line" once believed to be for the good of the student becomes a wedge driving the student and educator apart. The result often leads to the student being pushed out. Therefore, educators must move away from the appearance of imposed "hard-line" methods to an educational approach emphasizing their skills and abilities as professionals.

Instead of using gum rules and punishments as a means of teaching obedience, for example, why not approach the matter as an educator would—**teach students how to use gum properly**. Rather than pushing students out, gum could be used to build community and help students learn responsibility. For the most part, students learn responsibility only when they have something to be responsible for. They are far more likely to develop good character and become accountable for their behavior when they are respected as student/citizens capable of learning personal responsibility.

I remember an anecdote an elementary principal shared with me about his experience with "the gum problem." He had been a teacher in his building before being appointed principal and was familiar with the problem they had with gum damage. The custodian was constantly complaining about the wrappers on the floor and gum under the furniture. The punishments for chewing gum were harsh, but the problem continued.

When he became an administrator, one of his first acts was to revise some of the rules. One change in particular reversed the ban on gum chewing. His new plan suggested that the faculty spend some time during the first day of class teaching students how to use gum properly. Teachers instructed their classes in the appropriate way to chew gum, how to wrap it in paper when out of their mouths, where to discard the gum, and how to care for the empty wrapper.

Curious about the effect of this educational approach, a few weeks into the school year the principal asked the custodian if there was a problem with gum in the building. The custodian replied that he was surprised by the fact there was no gum anywhere around school, not even wrappers on the floor. "I don't know what you did," he said, "but you are the toughest principal we ever had here."

Another three weeks passed. The conversation again surfaced, and still no evidence of gum damage was found. "You really are tough," the principal was told, "What did you do?" The principal explained that the old rules were replaced by a more positive educational approach to teaching responsibility. The custodian listened in disbelief and, without a word, walked away shaking his head.

Too often educators react to misbehavior by simply trying to correct deficiencies rather than using long range educational approaches to help students change their goals and attitudes. When students waiver from educationally imposed boundaries, they need a mentor nearby, not a parent substitute or an authority figure to pull them back into line. Educators must approach discipline as professionals practicing what they have prepared themselves to do. When an academic or behavior problem does occur, it is an unswerving and dedicated educator who pauses to think—**"What needs to be learned here?"** Every student problem then becomes an educational challenge.

Formulating School Rules

Legal Implications

There are limits to the authority educators have when structuring rules appropriate to their educational responsibilities. Teachers, for example, may adopt any classroom rule they choose as long as it does not violate the rules of the principal, superintendent, school board, and state department of education. The classroom, school, or district structure cannot subtend state and federal legislative laws, the weight of state and federal case authority, or the United States Constitution. These are "the givens"—rules that are already in place and simply must be followed.

Faced with all the legislative and administrative strata, new teachers to a district may feel at a loss trying to locate and assimilate all the pertinent laws. These established rules and regulations are easily available, however, through a number of readily accessible sources. **First**, examine the state administrative laws affecting public education, available through state departments of education. These laws are most commonly referred to as state department administrative rules or codes. **Second**, investigate school board policies, usually available in the district office or school libraries.

Third, if there is a negotiated collective bargaining agreement, know the rules agreed upon by the teachers and the school board. **Fourth**, read your principal's rules regarding building policies and regulations relating to teacher responsibilities. **Lastly**, review a copy of the student handbook and know the rules affecting students in your building. Educators must know their boundaries and the rules they cannot change. It's hard to say this delicately, but violating any of these "givens" is called insubordination.

In a democracy, human rights can be limited by government to a reasonable **time, place,** and **manner**. For example, freedom of speech in a classroom does not mean students can speak up at any time or in any manner they choose. Students need to know that the responsibility that comes along with their constitutional right of free speech can be reasonably regulated by their teacher to the learning environment needs of the classroom.

The concept of time, place, and manner is a good organizer for groups to use as they learn to process the balancing of power. For example, a teacher could ask two students disrupting class by talking loudly to each other, "is this a reasonable time for this conversation?" or "can you think of a better place to talk?" Using the concepts of time, place, and manner gives form and substance to responsible behavior. The questions then focus on the reasonable behavior and away from the possibility of a power struggle with a demand of "stop the talking." Time, place, and manner can be used by teachers whenever there is a need to emphasize student responsibilities.

Often educators believe they are creating a democratic environment when they ask for a consensus from the class members or allow the group to vote on an issue. This is not always a good idea, nor does it accurately reflect our democratic principles. Students must understand that if the matter involves student rights, the question is simply not open to majority vote. Our democratic form of government only allows us to vote on those issues that are not protected by the Bill of Rights.

For example, if all the members of an athletic team vote to pray before each game, this group prayer would be in violation of the Establishment Clause of the First Amendment. Although there are those who will argue that everyone wants it that way, and no one is being hurt, constitutional rights also protect those who are not there. It would be difficult to determine, for example, how many students were discouraged from going out for the team because of a different religious tradition or even the fact that some on the team feel they must "pray to play." Human rights exist for the purpose of building community as well as keeping it open and inviting for all to join.

There are occasions, especially in the area of student privileges, when majority votes are appropriate and should be encouraged. For example, there should be no problem allowing students to decide which band will play at the dance, or whether to serve ice cream or popcorn at the class party.

Writing School Rules

School rules should be kept to a minimum. The four compelling state interests described previously provide a good outline to follow. They are easy for students to remember and for educators to manage.

However, if these four were the only rules, they would be unconstitutionally vague because of their breadth and, as a result, violate students' procedural due process rights to adequate notice. For instance, a general rule preventing property damage places students on notice not to damage the school, but is not specific enough as to what behavior would be injurious. It would not, for example, sufficiently inform students that the gym floor is more susceptible to damage from regular street shoes than the floors in the hallways and classrooms.

These initial broad headings should be followed by some specific examples of expected student behavior. This can be done either verbally or in writing and always with community involvement. The list need not be exhaustive, but should encompass a number of examples to facilitate awareness and understanding of the rules. These could include examples learned from past incidents as well as problem areas that could reasonably be anticipated. This two-pronged approach will address students who argue "the rules didn't cover that" as well as students who claim "I didn't know what you meant."

Crystal Schmidt-Dipaola, principal at Minter Bridge Elementary School in Hillsboro, Oregon, appointed a building CORE Team representing each grade level to develop building rules based on *Judicious Discipline*. The Team came up with the following recommendations for the whole Minter Bridge community:

1. Act in a Safe and Healthy Way

Use furniture appropriately, walk in the building and other designated areas, follow playground rules, follow bus riding rules, keep hands and feet to self. (Compelling State Interest: Health and Safety)

2. Treat All Property With Respect

Take care of textbooks, library books, school furniture, school bathrooms, computers, and personal property of others. Borrow the property of others ONLY after asking permission. (Compelling State Interest: Property)

3. Respect the Rights and Needs of Others

Work without disruption, show courtesy towards others, cooperate to help others learn, use appropriate language, feel good about yourselves. (Compelling State Interest: Serious Disruption of the Educational Process)

4. Take Responsibility for Learning

Strive for excellence, work hard and do your best, come to school prepared to learn, be a good listener, turn in your assignments on time, do your homework, keep track of your materials, set a

85

good example for others. (Compelling State Interest: Legitimate Educational Process)

Educators should work to develop rules that **emphasize the behavior desired** and empower students to think for themselves. For example, "move carefully in the halls" might replace "no running in the halls." Instead of "no street shoes on the gym floor," rules could be created that elicit responsible decision making such as "wear shoes that will not damage the gym floor." Reasons embodied in rules have the effect of trusting students to think for themselves as well as the appearance that the rule is not arbitrary.

By focusing on the appropriate behavior, it also avoids problems such as students who were bumping into people because they were walking backwards and then claiming they were abiding by the rule of "no running." Along the same lines, a swimming coach once told me that he would always yell "don't run, don't run" at students running near the pool. He said that with all the noise they would only hear the word "run." Not until he changed to yelling "walk, walk" did his message seem to get through. By clarifying, describing, and teaching positive behavior, educators can avoid the use of negative statements. The "do not" rules should be necessary only in case of potential danger or a compelling need for clarity.

Rules should be written clearly for the educational level of those affected. It is imperative that students fully understand the meaning of rules in order to meet the adequate notice requirement of the Fourteenth Amendment. "Ignorance of the law is no excuse" is a common phrase, but it has little application to students required to attend public schools. Almost all are minors, some with limited English-speaking ability, while others may have disabilities. Merely giving students a copy of the rules or posting them is not sufficient notice in many cases to allow legal enforcement.

The law does not require school authorities to state all of the rules in writing before school begins in the fall. Reasonable additions and deletions are allowed during the school year. The issue is whether the school can show cause for the rule change and whether students are given adequate notice. Any of the compelling state interests, however, should withstand this test of reasonable cause.

Philosophical Considerations

Philosophically speaking, democratic and autocratic classrooms approach rules from two entirely different directions. In democratic classrooms, rules would be based largely on the concept that students are free, but are denied their freedoms through their welfare responsibilities. In autocratic classrooms, rules begin with student responsibilities and privileges are earned through good behavior. The question is one of emphasis. Should educators place more importance on students' individual freedoms and the responsibilities that accompany them, or on rules that leave behaviors not covered by predetermined restrictions as being acceptable?

The approach chosen usually makes a significant difference in how students react to authority. For example, to err in an atmosphere of freedom, justice, and equality does not bring students down, but allows them to experience the price of learning responsibility. These students will become more motivated, capable, respectful, and independent. Conversely, to err in a classroom that emphasizes personal limitations tends to bring students down by discouraging their individuality. This creates a debilitating environment that causes students to be more unresponsive, defiant, insecure, and co-dependent. As a result, the philosophy adopted by educators directly affects the attitude and behavior of students.

Many schools that have adopted *Judicious Discipline* have found it helpful to begin the process by developing a philosophy statement of professional responsibilities. One of the first school groups to use this approach was the teachers and administrators of Cleveland High School in Portland, Oregon. The following statement of philosophy is used as a preamble to their student handbook. It reads as follows:

> Cleveland High School is a learning environment in which members of this community feel comfortable, challenged, and involved. The members of the Cleveland community are responsible to each other for behavior that exhibits an awareness of respect for human dignity and individual differences. Members of this community share the responsibility to maintain a safe climate that promotes and encourages learning.
>
> As members of this community, students have the right to know the rationale for the rules and decisions affecting them, a right to an equal educational opportunity, and an opportunity to participate in the procedures which ensure these rights. Students will lose these rights when their individual actions infringe on the rights or property of others.
>
> The primary goal of Cleveland High School is to prepare students to be contributing members of a society which uses a democratic process. Ultimately, Cleveland graduates will possess academic and social skills that will prepare them to function as responsible citizens.

The building rules, as well as each teacher's classroom rules, reflect this building philosophy. The principal, Robert O'Neill, also uses this statement as a basis for hiring new teachers as well as evaluating present staff members.

Another variation was developed by Charley Jones, director of the North Area Alternative Education Program in Salem, Oregon. The students in his program have dropped out or have been pushed out of mainstream public schooling. The language in his Mutual

Letter of Intent, with its emphasis on building community, is inviting, respectful, and designed to keep students in school. After students and their parents read the letter and discuss the program, they all sign it. Parts of this letter are as follow:.

NORTH AREA "CHOICES" MUTUAL LETTER OF INTENT

The "Choices" program is a learning community where members feel comfortable, involved, and bonded in a mutual educational goal. We believe in caring and sharing with each other. We believe in respecting the individual rights of our members and our community. We believe our community grows stronger with each new personality. The "lending and blending" of individual strengths through the respect of each of our members is the foundation of our program.

The members of our community share a common responsibility to maintain a safe learning environment and to respect community and individual property. Members are in jeopardy of losing their rights when their actions threaten the safety, rights, or property of another member. As members of our community we have a right to know the rationale for any disciplinary action that involves us as an individual.

...As members of "Choices" experience learning and behavior problems, every effort will be made to bring them back into the community. We believe that only through community support can our members get back on track. One person's absence will leave us weaker and he/she will be missed. Should any occurrence preclude a member's regular attendance, a leave of absence may be granted. The community will look forward to the member's return. All attendance matters will remain confidential and be based on individual and community needs.

...Congratulations! You have made a great "Choice." We are excited about having you as a member of our community. We look forward to your participation.

89

In summary, the student handbook and respective classroom rules are, for most students and parents, a first impression of the educational environment under which students will live and learn. Just and equitable rules that generate positive feelings go a long way to help alleviate fears that often accompany anticipated encounters with authority figures. For these reasons, the philosophy upon which all rules and decisions will be based is critical to whether school will be an inviting and safe place for students.

The First Day of Classes

Bringing about a feeling of community in a classroom begins with an educator's belief that all students are capable of proper social interaction. Activities on the first day that communicate trust in students' abilities to reason and to "stick by their word" is crucial in establishing boundaries necessary for a positive educational atmosphere. Ironically, it is not the rules that keep students in school and behaving appropriately, it is the philosophy and attitude with which educators approach rules that convinces students they belong in school.

Empowering students from the beginning is by far the most effective method of avoiding the bane of every educators' existence—power struggles. From the first day teachers meet their students the issue should be: how creatively and expeditiously can classroom power and authority be shared with students?

Imagine, for example, teachers beginning their first class with something like: "Good morning, students. Welcome to a classroom where your constitutional rights will be protected and balanced with the responsibilities that flow from those rights. As an example of what I mean, let's begin with your First Amendment right of freedom of the press that allows you the right to publish and distribute written material in this classroom. Let's begin with practicing how this right works. I would like everyone to get out a piece of paper and pencil and write a note to someone in this class. If you do not know someone, introduce yourself to your neighbor or write to me if you would like."

While students are writing notes to each other, something can be said about the importance of developing writing skills as well as getting to know someone in class. When students have finished writing, it is time to introduce the responsibilities that must be balanced with their freedom of the press. These responsibilities might be expressed something like the following:

"Now that you have all experienced what it means to have freedom of the press, let's talk about what responsibilities that right carries in our classroom. For example, what do you think would be a reasonable time, place, and manner for any of us to write a note during class time?" After some discussion, the next question could be: "What do you think would be a reasonable time, place, and manner for any of us to pass a note in this class?"

By experiencing responsibility through an act as universally forbidden as passing notes, students on their first day of class sense very quickly that something is different about the class. It is a class where teachers are sharing their power and students are learning the language of civility in a democratic classroom community. Not until teachers allow students to exercise their rights, even though they are occasionally abused, will students have the opportunity to learn and experience the responsibilities of living in a democracy. While not every teacher moving toward a democratic classroom may feel ready to begin a class this way, it is a good example of what educators can do with practice and experience using the concepts of *Judicious Discipline*.

Though it is preferable to devote adequate class time to rules and consequences, the logistics and practicality may vary greatly from one classroom to another. Self-contained classrooms where

91

students are together most of the day, all year long, present greater opportunities for student input and discussion than classes that meet once a day in forty or fifty minute sessions for part of the school year. Although strategies may differ, the goal of sharing ownership through teaching democratic principles remain the same.

Elementary Classes

In self-contained classrooms, teachers have a greater opportunity to employ an **inductive approach** to classroom rules and consequences. Two associates of mine, Barbara McEwan Landau, a professor of education, and Margaret Abbott, an elementary teacher and administrator, have been working with the concepts of *Judicious Discipline* and offer the following as an example of a lesson plan for elementary students using the inductive approach:

UNDERSTANDING RIGHTS AND CREATING RULES IN A DEMOCRATIC CLASSROOM

Objective: To inform students of their rights and when those rights are denied according to society's needs. To provide students with an opportunity to apply that information to the development of classroom rules.

Opening: "Take out a piece of paper and pencil. As fast as you can, write down all the individual rights you think you have in our country." (Put their responses on the board.) "Now, write down all the rights you think you have when you're in school." (Put these responses on the board.) "Would you be surprised to find out that your rights as citizens of our country and your rights in school are almost the same? Today we will be discussing the citizenship rights you have in a public school classroom and

92

when you can lose those rights. Understanding the rights we all have and knowing what actions can cause those rights to be denied helps us to become responsible citizens in school and in our society."

Procedure: Say to the students: "Let's look again at the rights we've put on the board. Let's see if there is a way to group them into categories. First, how do we know we have these rights? Who or what tells us that we do?"

Guide students through a brief review of the Constitution and Amendments: "In school you have all your rights protected. You even have more rights in a classroom than I do." (Use example of students wearing political buttons, but teachers refraining from such a statement.) "For the most part there are three amendments that are very important to remember in school: The First, Fourth, and Fourteenth."

Follow with a brief explanation of what these amendments include: "Who can tell me which of the rights on the board would come from the First Amendment? The Fourth? The Fourteenth?" (Teacher should fill in the gaps as needed.) "You are citizens in my classroom and I will treat you accordingly."

"I am a citizen in this town, state, and country. When I'm not in this classroom I am entitled to all of my rights. What does that mean? Does that mean I can do anything I want to? Can I do anything I feel like doing?"

Brainstorm and list on the board actions the teacher cannot do outside of the classroom: "When we put your rights on the board we were able to group them into different amendments. Let's look at your ideas about when I lose my rights and see if we can discover some headings those actions would fit under. In your groups of four, work together to see if you can find headings or categories for the situations on the board."

In five minutes check to see if they have discovered any patterns to the actions. Put up their ideas for categories and display a poster of the four Compelling State Interests. Briefly explain them: "When society denies my rights, they do it because of a Compelling State Interest. I can't throw a rock through a store window or run a red light or yell fire in a theater. As citizens in this classroom you will lose your rights if I can show a Compelling State Interest applies to something you are doing. Let's look again at the compelling state interests. In your groups take a few minutes to discuss what actions students might engage in that would result in them losing their rights because of a compelling state interest."

In five minutes bring groups back together to share their ideas: "Now that you have an understanding of what rights you have and when those rights can be denied, let's think together how we can use this information to develop rules for our class. What rules could we develop that would match each one of the compelling state interests? What would be a reasonable classroom rule to reflect property loss and damage?" Work through each of the compelling state interests.

Closing: "Now that we have discussed your citizenship rights and developed classroom rules based on the compelling state interests, we are ready for the next step. Tomorrow we will talk about Judicious Consequences. You will learn what they are and help to create consequences for our classroom that are fair and make sense."

Margie Abbott had been teaching fifteen years before she began to use *Judicious Discipline*. She had always started the year by asking her fourth grade students what rules they thought they needed for their classroom. Over the years, many different rules were implemented, but she always felt a need for an organizer to bring them all together.

Once Margie implemented *Judicious Discipline*, the wording for the rules came from the students after each compelling state interest was explained and understood. Time was spent

94

discussing the intent of the rules, the significance of each, and the concerns students expressed. Questions were encouraged to eliminate uncertainty. When the rules were clearly understood, they were posted in the classroom. All students then signed the rules poster, agreeing to follow them to the best of their ability.

Although the rules the students came up with would change slightly from year to year, the following is an example of one set of her classes' rules based on the four compelling state interests:

1. Respect other people's property. (property loss and damage)
2. We are here to listen and learn. (legitimate educational purpose)
3. Conduct yourself in a safe manner and be healthy. (health and safety)
4. Be yourself and respect others. (serious disruption)

Teachers working with younger students have been very successful teaching the principles of democracy by using language and examples to which their children really can relate. For example, they will use the word "choices" along with the word "rights" when they are teaching the concept of human rights. They often use stuffed animals to represent students and a scale to show the balance between one stuffed animal and the other animals. The children really enjoy talking about the responsibilities that come along with their right to choose. Head Start and day care teachers have been very resourceful and creative in finding ways to create a democratic community. Learning responsibility begins with students talking and making decisions for their own responsible behavior.

Secondary Classes

Secondary educators meeting five or six classes a day for forty to fifty minutes each not only feel pressured by time constraints on the first day, but also need consistent sets of rules for all their classes. These teachers, therefore, are more likely to employ a **deductive approach** to establishing classroom rules and consequences.

Traditionally, secondary teachers have used their course outline or syllabus as the basis of establishing their teaching philosophy. Because of this, most secondary teachers integrate *Judicious Discipline* into these outlines. They usually use these on the first day to elaborate on their expectations and consequences of student behavior. Questions and discussion that follow create a sense of empowerment and responsibility on the part of students. Involving the students in a dialogue of reasons brings about a sense of agreement for the academic and behavioral expectations of the syllabus. Although secondary students would not be actively engaged in developing their classroom rules, course expectations and consequences nevertheless acknowledge and embrace their human rights.

Although most secondary teachers use the deductive approach, Bill Howry, an English teacher at Corvallis High School in Corvallis, Oregon, found the inductive process worked very well for him. The following is his narrative of how he begins his classes:

> After teaching high school students for nineteen years, I have just completed my most successful year in the business. In the middle of June, my students and I are still enjoying a mutual respect, and most of us feel that the year has been not only enjoyable, but worthwhile. A large part of this success stems from a two-week unit I conducted in mid-September.
>
> Following a few days of diagnostic testing, I opened the class one

day with a proposal that since we were in this together and for the duration, perhaps we needed some guidelines to coexist by. Freshmen are fairly used to rules being imposed on them, and, being new to the high school system, they were willing to listen to any I had concocted for them. Instead, I asked them to come up with their own set of rules. This excited some and worried others. I asked them to work in small groups to compose the ten most necessary guidelines to live by in our classroom.

Surprisingly enough, all groups seriously attacked the assignment. After fifteen groups (from all three of my Freshman English classes) had turned in their lists, I compiled a composite list to hand back to them. Here are the top ten, including the number of times each rule appeared on any list:

(6) 1. Do not distract others from their work.
(4) 2. Chewing gum is allowed.
(4) 3. Students may discuss assignments with each other.
(4) 4. Respect the teacher and your classmates.
(3) 5. Students may write notes or do other homework if finished with the day's assignments.
(3) 6. Do not talk in a loud, disruptive manner.
(3) 7. Do not talk while the teacher is talking.
(2) 8. Students are allowed to leave class for a good reason.
(2) 9. Always bring study materials (books, pencil, paper) to class.
(2) 10. Raise your hand before speaking.

Other rules that appeared on lists included keeping one's hands to oneself, being able to wear hats and sunglasses, not running in the classroom, and being assured that the teacher would not confront a student in front of the class. When I handed the composite list back to them (25 rules in all), no one seemed too surprised at the absolute tone or the large number of rules.

I then asked them to lay the list aside for a few days and to take notes on what I was about to tell them. Being new to both me and the system, they were amenable to this, too.

The next few days were spent in discussion (using an overhead projector to emphasize certain words and concepts) of the principles of *Judicious Discipline*. I began with the concept of balance: the rights of the majority and the freedoms of individuals. I discussed the basic values of freedom, justice, and equality. We overviewed the First, Fourth, and Fourteenth Amendments, focusing on the Fourteenth. I gave them a new term and, for many, a new concept: compelling state interest. We covered each state interest, discussing examples for each. I provided them with some landmark cases; they came up with some interesting hypothetical cases of their own.

Finally, being fairly sure that they understood the concept of compelling state interest, I asked them to take out their list of rules for a second look. We proceeded through the list, evaluating each rule against the compelling state interest categories. Students were quick to see whether each of their rules was compatible with the concept of compelling state interest.

Immediately following this discussion, I gave them an outline of guidelines I consider fair. Since the guidelines I suggested were based on what we had just spent four days talking about, there was practically no discussion. I suspected that they were willing to give the system a try.

Now, in June, I feel that they actually did try. I followed through with the policies of due process in grading and behavior matters. I kept an open gradebook and an open mind. I confronted students occasionally, but not in front of their peers. While other factors may have contributed to the cause, I am sure of the effect. I had fewer tardies and other discipline problems than I have had in the past ten years. I had few problems with late papers. I was delighted much more often than I was disappointed. And I have seen the students reach goals I really didn't think possible at the beginning of the year.

Because of the nature of their job, **substitute teachers** experience more "first days of class" than anyone in education. It is common knowledge that the success of every substitute is directly related to their ability to establish a good rapport with students in the first few minutes. Carol Griffith, a substitute teacher who had taken one of my classes, was sharing with me how she begins class each time she substitutes. She told me that her first words to the class are "I'm Ms. Griffith and I am here to protect your constitutional rights." Student response, she said, ranges from quiet and surprised to that of interested and intrigued.

Carol told me that she feels problems arise when substitutes are either afraid of the students or the students are made to fear the substitute. But by using the word "rights" and announcing from the very beginning her professional responsibilities, she produces an immediate calming effect that alleviates fears and establishes mutual trust. After that, everything else she does is consistent with "the balance" and student behavior is never a problem. She ended by telling me that not only does she really enjoy substituting, but principals call her all the time now for help in difficult classes.

The way educators use their authority goes to the very heart of their professional responsibility. Because "the law" is such a powerful force when used by authority figures against misbehaving students, it often has a debilitating effect on their attitude toward school. But how much more effective our schools could be in preparing students to live in America if we would teach and model the civil rationale for society's boundaries along with values of tolerance and responsible compliance to democratic principles. Only then will students have an opportunity to experience the joys and sorrows of being accountable for their own actions.

⚖

Class Meetings

At the core of constitutional freedoms is the First Amendment right "...of the people peaceably to assemble, and to petition the government for a redress of grievances." What better, well-grounded principle on which to base class meetings than the Constitution. If teachers would teach students about their constitutional right to speak out in this public forum, it would certainly give new meaning and importance to class meetings.

Class meetings are important because they create among students a sense of enfranchisement. They have the effect of giving students a sense of significance as well as having some control over what happens in school.

Rules decided on at the beginning of the year often need clarification or require reconsideration due to some unforseen event. Meetings also offer an opportunity for students and teachers to bring up new subjects for discussion, such as classroom ethics. In addition, student violations of rules can be brought up for group discussion, instead of denouncing students individually. It is also not uncommon for students to want to meet occasionally just to reinforce their need to feel their questions and opinions are still valued. Just having an opportunity to speak out is crucial to the well-ordered functioning of any democratic community.

The success of class meetings is related directly to the ability of teachers to help students see all sides of the issues presented by asking the relevant questions and then listening. Students who are talking are being empowered as they gain a sense of authority and its accompanying responsibilities. Allowing students to experience some authority over what happens to them in class eliminates almost all of the reasons students resort to "power struggles." This proactive approach for dealing with issues of power and civil morality often resolves problems before they get started.

Conversely, if class meetings are called by teachers in order to lecture or chastise students, they become a thinly veiled means of asserting authority, missing completely their intended purpose of shared authority and mutual respect.

An example of shared authority was recently related to me by a high school English teacher who freely admitted to having the worst seventh period class in seventeen years of teaching. The students would come in talking and would not settle down. She told me they wanted to talk all the time and that she spent much of the period quieting them down and keeping them on task. Completely frustrated with her previous strategies, she decided on a class meeting.

She started the meeting by saying: "You all seem to enjoy talking with each other so why don't we take some time during the period to do that. Would you like five minutes at the beginning, in the middle, or at the end?" After a brief discussion among themselves, the students decided on five minutes of talking in the middle of the class period. Since then, she told me, the students come in and, with only a reminder or two, get right to work. They really looked forward to their five minutes of talking before getting back on task. Besides alleviating her frustration, giving up five minutes of class time has more than made up for the time she had spent getting and keeping their attention. Now, she said, they seldom remember their talking time and are on task the whole period.

The following are some key elements for conducting democratic class meetings. These were developed by Paul Gathercoal based on his research and experience working with students and techers in their classrooms.

Some Key Elements
for Conducting Democratic Class Meetings

◆ **Determine who can call a class meeting and when they should be held. What is a proper time, place, and manner?** Some teachers allow any student in the class to call a class meeting whenever one is necessary. Other teachers determine a specific time, place, and manner. Both methods and a variety of methods in-between can work well as along as the calling of a class meeting has the effect of giving students a sense of significance and some power and control over what happens in their classroom. The important element is that democratic class meetings will occur and that there is some mechanism for calling a class meeting to order.

◆ **All students and the teacher should be seated so everyone can see the faces of the others in the class meeting**. How we position ourselves says much about power relationships.

To instill a sense of significance and power in the students, **sit in a circle or square shape where everyone can communicate easily with any other person in the class meeting**. The physical environment in the classroom should be as *inclusive* as possible, and students and teachers who sit comfortably in a closed circle provide for a feeling of community that encourages positive and productive communication. The more "formal" physical arrangements (sitting in rows) have the effect of excluding students, or allowing students to exclude themselves. This feeling of exclusion may occur for other reasons, e.g., name-calling, or an individual's posture within the circle; but, by sitting in a circle, the physical environment is optimized and communication is amplified.

◆ **Set the expectations that we will never use names during the class meeting**. Using names casts an accusatory finger at the person being named and has the effect of putting that person on the defense. It also causes ill feelings. Negotiate with students not to use class members' names. Ask, "How would you feel if everyone in the class was talking about you?" Most students would feel embarrassed and defensive. Suggest that when talking about problems and behaviors that the class should talk in terms of, "a person who acts this way..." rather than, "When (Person's Name) acts like..." This protects individuals in the class and allows them to participate in the discussions about behavior and not about personalities.

◆ **Set the expectations that we will stay on the toic and carefully guard any sharing about our families during the class meetings**. The efficiency of any class meeting is mediated by the class' ability to stay on topic and to discuss all agenda items with an open mind. By guarding carefully what is brought to the attention of the meeting and by keeping the topic free of "family or personal concerns," the class meeting is more likely to flow quickly and smoothly.

◆ **The teacher should lead the class meeting**. Our action research indicates that when teachers hand over the leadership role to students, the class meeting digresses. Many teachers think having "Class Officers" and empowering them with the administrative power to lead the meeting is "in line" with democratic principles and that the practice leads students to autonomy. In fact, our research findings indicate the opposite. The whole process of deciding and empowering "Class Officers" propogates popularity contests and competition. These contests generate ill feelings and can result in a major breakdown in community building and in students' achievement of the autonomous stages of social development. **There should be one educational leader in the classroom and that is the teacher**. The teacher needs to conduct the democratic class meeting.

◆ **Students should never be coerced to participate in the class meeting**. It is a good idea to set the expectation that it is okay to "pass" if an individual chooses not to contriobute to the discussioon.

◆ **It is a good idea for each student and teacher to have a personal class meeting journal**. In this journal the teacher and students can write down their thoughts and goals. Even kindergarten students can record their thoughts in a journal. Often the younger students will record their thoughts in picture form. This is okay; it is a powerful feeling when students view themselves as writers and readers of their own journal entries.

It is important that the teacher participates by writing in his or her personal journal. This sends a strong message to the students that this is important work; so important that the students' writing will be valued along with the teacher's writing.

A good way to begin class meetings is to write in your personal journal for a few minutes. This writing can occur at the beginning of the class meeting or at the end of the class meeting, and it can take place in small groups or be done individually. It is a good idea to vary the format, small groups one meeting, and individually the next.

Give guidelines or categories for writing in the personal journals and display these guidelines for all to see. You may want to change the guidelines or categories from week to week. Some guidelines or categories that have worked well are: "Concerns, Clarifications, and Delights," or "Something I'd Like To Talk about, Something I'd Like To Work on, and Things That Are Going Well." Using three categories and encouraging everyone to write at least one thing in each category works well. Always ensure that one of the categories allows students to raise issues that are problem areas, another category allows for questions, and the third category encourages celebrations and the acknowledgment of success.

After everyone has had time to write in their personal journal, assemble in a circle and use the personal journal entries as the agenda for the democratic meeting. Begin by asking, "Does anyone have concerns or clarifications they would like to discuss?" Save the "Delights" for the end of the meeting; they tend to make everyone feel good and do much to build community in the classroom.

◆ **It is a good idea for the students and the teacher to write down the goals they set for themselves after or during the class meeting**. The teacher and students can use their class meeting personal journal to write down goals they set for themselves. It is important that individuals set their own goals. No one should ever set a goal for someone else. It's okay to pose possible goals as questions, "What do you think about setting a goal like, ...?" But, to set a goal for someone else again brings about a co-dependent relationship and diminishes the mentoring relationship.

Writing down goals is important. Verbalizing goals accomplishes several things. It gives us something to strive for that is in a form we can visualize. It encourages us to take ownership in problem solving; and it gives us a measuring stick for our personal growth and performance in life. Writing the goal down is important, but sharing the goal with others is another matter.

Never direct members of the class to share their goals or musings in their personal journals with others. If they choose to share their goals, that is fine, but some goals may be more personal than others, and it is not for anyone else to decide what is personal and what is not. For example, one student may write the goal, "I need to start listening better." If this goal is shared with others, then others may taunt the goal-setter with, "You need to listen better!" and this can cause ill feelings and will not help the goal-setter to make an honest self-assessment or encourage him or her to set more goals in the future. In fact, you may want to warn your students, "It's important to write your goals down (and cite the reasons above as to why it is important), but be careful who you share your goals with and be sure and celebrate when you accomplish the goals you set for yourself."

Self-assess the goals individuals have set. The teacher can ask, "How are we going with the goals we set last meeting?" Without iterating the goal, the teacher and students can verbally self-assess, "I'm doing pretty good" or "I'm having some trouble with my goal." This allows the class to celebrate with those who achieve their goals and to offer moral support for those who may not be achieving as much as they think they should. Note that at no time does the person have to state what his or her goal is, they just offer an assessment of their progress. As with other agenda items, the teacher and students should all have the right to "pass" if they do not wish to self-assess their goals.

From the first day of class through the rest of the school year, class meetings can serve as the lifeblood of a democratic community. Whether class meetings occur on a regular basis or are called by teachers or students for a specific purpose, a forum for discourse and opinion on the changing dynamics of classroom life is one the most effective vehicles for sharing responsibility. The right to "...petition the government for a redress of grievances" is a powerful manifestation of mutual respect between students and teachers.

In summary, a democracy is designed to create a social contract between an individual student and the other members of the school community. As rules are discussed and developed around this new constitutional language of freedom, justice, and equality and the four compelling state interests, a participatory community culture is beginning to take shape. These new words and images forming in students' minds are the foundation of a democratic cultural environment. Only when members of a community have a sense of self-efficacy is democracy working as it was designed to work.

The power of this social contract was brought home to me by an incident related to me by an elementary principal whose school had just adopted *Judicious Discipline*. About three weeks into the school year, a bus driver told her about a boy on his bus who was pushing and teasing a third-grade girl. As the girl was trying to defend herself, she shouted back "you can't do that to me, that's health and safety." At that, the boy stopped and took his seat in the bus. The driver expressed surprise, because in his experience this boy never backed off when a girl asked him to stop. The principal explained that all the children in the school had been working with these democratic principles, and that was presumably the basis for the boy's behavior.

The difference between telling someone "you can't do that" and telling them "you can't do that..." followed by society's rationale "...that's health and safety" is significant. When the girl reminded the boy of the health and safety issue, it was more than just **her** command to stop; it was as though the **whole school community** was behind her, telling him that his behavior was in violation of the principle of another student's welfare. When everyone in the school community knows the language of civility and participates in the reasons for and formulation of rules, they are far more likely to abide by those rules and advocate for themselves by using that language to resolve their own problems.

In review, there are ten basic principles which comprise the framework for the values of civility and a judicious school enrivonment. On one side of the scale of justice are the basic principles of individual **freedom**, **justice**, and **equality**. The other side represents the welfare needs of the student body and are the four compelling state interests—**property loss and damage**, **legitimate educational purpose**, **health and safety**, and **serious disruption**. Providing the bridge for balancing these constitutional principles is the question of **reasonable time**, **place**, and **manner**.

Educators operating at a principled level of thinking and speaking are using these ten principles as their center for teaching and discussion. These provide the guidelines for "democratic talk" and the language for schools to create a comunity of civility, tolerance, and student responsibility.

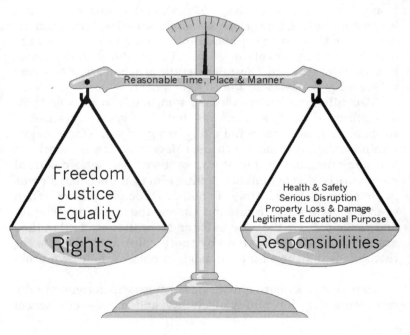

Reasonable Time, Place & Manner

Freedom
Justice
Equality
Rights

Health & Safety
Serious Disruption
Property Loss & Damage
Legitimate Educational Purpose
Responsibilities

CHAPTER 5:
CONSEQUENCES—
A PROFESSIONAL
RELATIONSHIP MODEL

Rules serve the purpose of providing boundaries and are effective only until they are broken. When students waiver from judiciously imposed boundaries, they need a professional educator nearby who is able to guide and support their recovery. A professional educator and mentor is someone who acts as a wise, loyal friend and advisor; one who helps lead students to finding their best selves, not by making them dependent, but by deepening their confidence in their abilities to own solutions. When a behavior problem does occur, it is a dedicated mentor/educator who pauses to think—"What does the student need to do now to rebuild the damage and what can be learned from what happened?" Every student's problem then becomes an educational opportunity.

If educators would direct their thoughts and efforts toward a professional relationship approach by utilizing mentoring strategies as the way to resolve problems, students would not be as likely to perceive themselves as being treated unreasonably. For example, when students make academic mistakes, good teachers use these mistakes for diagnostic purposes and employ effective educational strategies to help students overcome their learning difficulties. Professional educators are usually patient and understanding with students and know that academic accomplishments take some time to develop. It would only follow then, that the same professional approach toward behavior problems would be equally as effective.

Judicious Consequences

When a rule is broken, educators usually begin thinking in one of two completely different directions: (1) How shall I confront this student with the infraction and what would be the most appropriate punishment? or (2) What more do I need to know about this situation and which educational strategies will be most effective for bringing about a reasonable resolution? Each of the two mindsets conjures up various scenarios, at times mutually exclusive, and each eventually becomes the basis of new expectations as consequences are played out.

To many educators, the first may appear to be the more reasonable approach; the violation of rules followed by "an eye for an eye" type of punishment would seem to represent a logical extension of the justice model. After all, isn't justice what *Judicious Discipline* is all about? Contradictory as it may seem, judicious consequences for misbehavior are exactly where the justice model must be abandoned and a completely different approach must be used—that of a professional relationship.

Although the principles of justice work well in the development of fair and just rules, the justice model carried over to consequences may work as a detriment to educators seeking to change attitudes of misbehaving students. Within the criminal/justice system, for example, offenders are punished by sending them to jail, or in the case of a student at school, sending them to detention. Being treated as criminals and isolated from others would be exactly what students in trouble do not need.

Students experiencing problems are already feeling insecure, and they do not need educators compounding their problems by making them feel even more insecure. Rather, such students need help and support to resolve their problems in ways that will increase their feelings of self-worth. The criminal/justice system is traditionally society's last resort for resolving community problems and is used by our government only after everything else fails. Therefore, it does not make sense for educators to use the criminal/justice model first, before employing what they were professionally prepared to use—educational and mentoring approaches. Consequences then become ways for students to learn responsibility, rather than predetermined acts designed for retribution or to foster obedience.

I have discovered that I am most successful in establishing a professional relationship with students in trouble when I try to visualize their situations in broader terms than what appears to be the immediate problem. The following are some mental images I use that help me gain a broader perspective: (1) If I am this student's educator and mentor, I had better listen and act as his or her loyal friend and advisor; and (2) I must keep in mind that this student is not finished yet, but is in the process of growing to adulthood; and, therefore, (3) I must decide what I can do **now** to help him or her recover and learn something from an error in judgment.

Simply stated, I try to filter everything else out of my mind and make every effort to keep a focus on my responsibility as a professional. If I begin to think about my biases, I have a tendency to judge students' misbehavior and lose my concentration on the important issues of students' success and well-being. I am most effective when my energy is directed toward students in a concentrated effort, sincerely trying to help them process their feelings and understand their responsibilities.

The nature of judicious consequences embodies an holistic approach and implies a resolution that balances all ramifications and possibilities. It begins with identifying issues central to students' emotional development and educational needs in order to determine the compatibility of the educator's professional practices. It involves such questions as:

1. What needs to be learned here?
2. What is my role as a mentor/educator in resolving the problem?
3. Do I need more information about the events surrounding the problem?
4. What strategies can I use to get this student to talk about the problem?
5. How will the student perceive what I am trying to do; i.e., help with recovery, punish the misbehavior, etc.?
6. How will the problem's resolution affect the other members of the school community?
7. **And**, in order for the important issues of the problem to unfold and for workable solutions to take form; how can I keep intact the mutual respect needed for a strong professional relationship?

A judicious style, therefore, would be exemplified as wisdom blended with authority to make decisions and act upon them, but only after pivotal questions have been considered and the real issues have emerged. The move away from "autocratic talk" to communicating respect and dignity flows logically from asking "judicious questions." Engaging students in discourse is a strategy that ultimately empowers both students and educators through the role each plays in the school community.

⚖

Responding Professionally

If asked to retitle *Judicious Discipline*, I would call it something like, *How, When, Why, and Where to Back Off*. This is not to be confused with backing down or inaction, but simply using an approach that weighs all sides of the question so that responses can be tailored to ease into the most important problems. Instead of trying to be too inventive or manipulative, educators should learn the technique of "backing off." Often, this provides the space necessary for everyone to process the incident and see it in a new light. Time also allows other forces to be brought to bear upon the matter, letting many situations simply play themselves out.

Sometimes educators exacerbate a situation and a "me against them" mentality develops. For example, a flippant response by a teacher to the verbal threats of a student, such as "is that a threat or a promise?," is in essence a counter attack by an authority figure that immediately escalates the confrontation. Whatever is said next by either party is usually the language antagonists express to each other. Rather, confrontive students need someone in authority on their side; they need to hear something like: "It sounds like you are upset. Would you like to get together and talk about it?"

Talking about the problem after some "cool down" time would not be backing down or avoiding the issue, but rather allowing students time to process what they have done as well as creating an opportunity for a private meeting. In times of trouble, students need support and need to believe that educators are really working in their best interests.

It is very important that when a disruption does occur the first reaction be that of a professional educator acting in the best interests of the student. That is consistent with our professional preparation and responsibility, and is hopefully what we do best. The following illustration will emphasize the point.

Imagine the front of a classroom filled with adults who impact student lives. Standing there may be a teacher, parent, counselor, coach, principal, religious leader, a law enforcement officer, a children's services worker, a juvenile court judge, a college admissions officer, and an employer.

Now, with all of these people present, a confrontive student from the back of the classroom shouts at the teacher: "You '(expletive).' You gave me a D on my test."

Stereotyped responses from some of the people standing in the front of the room might sound something like the following: parents might lecture their confrontive child about how profanity conflicts with their family values; counselors would identify underlying causes and work on changing attitudes; religious leaders might preach about morality issues; coaches could be worried about losing a player; principals might consider a suspension; and so on down the list.

In this crowd of people witnessing this moment of public defiance, what role should the teacher play? The answer is—that of a professional classroom teacher. If that teacher is the student's best chance for academic success at that grade level or in that subject, the trust and care of a professional relationship simply must be kept intact. To accomplish this, the primary task of the teacher, then, is to avoid the pitfalls of trying to assume the roles of the other adults in the room.

The teacher's response to the student, then, might be something like: "Sounds like you are really having a bad day. Do you want to talk about this now or can it wait until class is over?" The message would be clear to all that the teacher is sincerely interested in the welfare of the upset student as well as with the importance of continuing on with the class. With this kind of "recognition" response, the teacher would not be backing down

114

nor condoning the student's behavior, but exemplifying the professional demeanor and the empathy necessary to keep intact a strong student/educator relationship. In addition, by responding with a question, the teacher allows the student to retain some power in the relationship. Just as with establishing rules, if consequences are to be effective in changing attitudes and behaviors, students must have some authority over their actions in the life of the consequences.

With practice in using this approach, educators will begin to look past rude and offensive language directed at them. Instead, each student's behavior, no matter how disruptive, will be perceived as an indication that something is wrong and the teacher will respond by going **indirectly** to what needs to happen next.

In contrast, educators who abandon their role of "professional teacher" by stepping into one of the other roles actually diminish their teaching integrity and eventually their effectiveness in the student/educator relationship. For example, teachers who attempt to parent students, preach to them about religious values, or warn them about future college and employment disasters, usually experience a sigh and rolling of the eyes, flippant wisecracks, argumentative comebacks, or any number of other "turn off" mechanisms that students use to distance themselves from talking authority figures.

When educators lose their students this way, students lose their educators, and students become the real losers. Classroom teachers are the student's best and sometimes their only chance for success in a given subject or grade level. For this reason alone, educators must avoid assuming the roles of others and keep pure a relationship that fosters a continuing rapport and confidence. Although troublesome students often leave classrooms for a short period of time, they usually come back. When the educational relationship is kept healthy and students believe they have not lost a teacher, returning students will always feel welcomed back.

Very important when developing a professional relationship is setting the stage properly. The handling of student problems usually occurs on the educator's turf. It is, therefore, important that a cordial invitation is extended to students. Educators coming around desks greeting students, as they would another adult, is a sign of respect. Something like "come on in—it looks like we have something to talk about" quickly establishes the importance of the students' worth and clearly invites conversation. Without a genuine invitation to conversation, trying to "develop the question" can quickly turn into a lecture.

Although educators make every effort to make their office or classroom inviting, some students are unwilling to discuss matters there. One approach is to meet these students at a neutral site, or even on their own "turf," much like making house calls. This more balanced playing field for discussion often relaxes students enough to let them open up and get to the real problem. Offices and classrooms can sometimes be threatening and intimidating places for students who are unsure about themselves in the school environment.

The concept of territory is powerful and one that students can understand at an early age. At an elementary school I recently visited, the school counselor showed me a room set aside just for play therapy. Students who were experiencing problems could come there under his supervision to play out many of their feelings of frustrations. The counselor would often invite parents to come play with their children as a way to provide a setting where children could feel they were on their own "turf" and that their parents were in the role of their guests. Because the students felt some control in their school setting, this was the first time for most of the families involved where children and parents learned how to really talk with each other.

Thoughtful approaches to problem resolution help give students confidence that they are in the hands of competent educators. A hammer or a chisel can be very useful tools for resolving some building construction problems, but other jobs require the delicate manipulation of tiny Phillips screwdrivers or needle-nosed pliers. Educators should not try to use a hammer to solve every classroom problem, but carry a tool box filled with strategies and ideas for the purpose of mentoring students.

When educators run out of workable ideas, they often lose their patience and have a tendency to "take it out on their students." On the other hand, educators with a tool box of ideas are professionals with patience and self-assurance.

Developing the Question

The first words spoken to a student who has misbehaved should be in the form of a question. It avoids accusatory statements and lectures and immediately begins the healing process by sending a powerful message that you are acting in the best interests of the student. Accusations and lectures push the student away, whereas beginning with questions gives the student power in the relationship The person talking not only has the power, but the responsibility for what is said. In every other professional relationship, the professionals ask questions and their clients do the talking before any decisions are made.

Physicians, for example, would not prescribe automatically two aspirin to every patient who complains of feeling ill. Rather, physicians respond to medical problems with: "Where does it hurt?" "How long has it been that way?" and "Is it worse when I do this?" Before a lawyer agrees to represent anyone, considerable time is taken pursuing the facts and interests of the client. Without gathering appropriate and relevant information, professionals simply cannot act in the best interests of the people they are employed to serve. Just as with other professional fields,

117

educators must learn to approach discipline problems by asking the relevant professional questions.

Behavioral problems should be approached by asking general questions of inquiry and concern in an effort to encourage students to talk about what **they** perceive happened. "Coming to the point" does not mean beginning with an accusatory statement. It means approaching the problem from the **perspective of the student** with the intent of getting to the heart of the problem. Asking "what happened?" or "is there something I can do to help?" or offering a descriptive statement like "it looks like you might be having a bad day—would you like to talk about it?" usually prompts students to open up and discuss the problem.

The focus of the conversation must be away from students defending who they **are** to encouraging them to talk about what they have **done**. Therefore, always avoid asking students "**why**?" questions. "**What** happened?" or "Would you like to talk about **it**?" focus on what and it, thereby separating students from their acts. This strategy is essential for students to feel educators are acting in the students' best interests. When educators appear to students to be on the students' side, a professional relationship replaces the adversarial relationship.

Students who are in trouble usually know the rules and are aware that they have messed up. Given the opportunity to speak with an educator they trust to be working in their best interests, many students, on their own volition, will bring up the infraction and be quite willing to talk about it. Students who are talking about how they perceive their misbehavior in relation to the situation are beginning to take ownership of the problem, and, if properly handled, will eventually become accountable for their actions.

A good example is an anecdote related to me by a teacher in one of my week-long workshops. She had been experiencing problems with her five year old son leaving his coat in the car when returning home. She would tell him "get your coat." He would respond with "you get it." They would then argue about responsibility and who should get it. One night, she told me, her son left his coat in the car again so she decided to try the "question approach" she learned in the workshop. Instead of her usual command, all she said was "what about your coat?" And he said "I'll get it, mommy." The teacher could not believe the answer to her problem could be as simple as changing from "telling" to "asking" her son about his coat.

Questions have a way of "softening the blow" to someone who might be in the wrong, and allow them some space to save face and recover. It also gets educators away from sounding threatening or accusatory, which helps keep intact a mentoring relationship. For example, a teacher who says "this answer is wrong" tends to create a defensiveness in students. But a teacher who asks "does this answer look right to you?" softens the error and immediately empowers students to take responsibility in the recovery process.

By asking leading questions and listening carefully, the underlying issues begin to emerge. Professionals in every field get very adept at asking leading questions based on their expertise and intuition. "Professional probing" can take many forms, such as personal reactions, interested inquiries, or even a shared opinion on the subject. For example, students caught cheating on a test do not need a lecture on morality, but rather an opening response such as: "What happened? Could it be that you did not have adequate time to prepare for the test?"

Also, during the probing period, a well-placed "tell me what you have decided to do about that" keeps the focus on just who is accountable and in charge of the resolution.

Just changing the approach from "I am in charge here" to that of mutual expectations improves communications immediately. For example, "can I expect your term project to be completed before I must turn in your grade?" might replace: "You had better get busy on your term project. You know it is due by the end of the term." Another example would be "I expect we should talk sometime soon about your test last week?" which could replace a demanding statement such as "you had better see me soon about your poor performance on last weeks' test."

Expectations that replace limits and demands have the effect of showing respect for students' judgment. It is a strong message to students that they have significant control in their education as well as the responsibility of an equal partner in mutual expectations.

Students who do not respond to questions immediately, or who refuse to discuss the situation, often need more time to process their feelings. When faced with stubborn attitudes, educators should not force the conversation, but instead say something like: "I see that you would rather not discuss this now. Maybe we can get together later, when we both have had time to think about it." In many cases, students need some time to get past the hurt or embarrassment they feel before they are ready to talk.

Whether it is about misbehavior, a request for advice, or even support for something done well, educators want to say the right thing, not something that will discourage students. Experience has taught me that the "right" response is not nearly as important as having an empowering attitude. If educators are focused on listening, discourse leading to positive interaction tends to flow easily. With such an attitude, it seems that no matter what is said, it will be interpreted by students positively and teachers will be perceived as acting in their best interests.

In summary, something as simple as leading questions and listening become a strategy that can be used over and over again with the same powerful effectiveness—that of empowering students. Good communication lies not in the words we use, but in the spaces between the words. The longer the spaces, the more we are sharing power with our students. As a result, the more authority students have over their life, the more they are accountable for their own thoughts and actions. For students to believe in their educators and look to them as loyal friends and advisors is not by any means a given; it is something that must be earned everyday.

Shaping Consequences

Engaging students in classroom discussions of possible future consequences before problems arise is an important aspect of *Judicious Discipline*. Although judicious consequences should not be predetermined for each future misbehavior, students do have a right to know what kinds of consequences they can expect to be discussing with their teachers when it comes to minor and major infractions of the rules. Previously discussed consequences, therefore, give students and teachers a kind of "ballpark figure" starting place when it comes time to sit down and work things through. If students are involved in discussing consequences to rule violations, they will not only feel a shared ownership, but are far more likely to accept their responsibility when or if the time should come.

An educator's approach to shaping consequences should reflect the basic principles of empowerment and student responsibility and avoid forcing explanations from students about what is already past. Students should know that when rules have been broken, their discussion with educators will center around two important future aspects: (1) **What needs to be done now?** and (2) **What can we learn from this?**

"What needs to be done now?" usually involves two concepts, **restitution** and an **apology**. Both are designed to make things right by bringing the situation back whole again. For example, when a student is caught taking something from another student, the leading questions center around restitution of the property and a discussion of an appropriate apology. By focusing on just two aspects intended to restore property and feelings, educators can avoid the negative effects of punishment and focus on empowering strategies to make things whole again. Students and educators will not get mired down in superficial arguments of right and wrong which are not constructive to successfully resolving the issue.

While "what needs to be done now?" is meant to take care of the past, "what can we learn from this?" is directly related to the educator's commitment to changing future goals and attitudes of students. An educator's ability to enhance students feeling of self-worth as a result of a negative experience is truly an art form.

When students experiencing difficulties are in the capable hands of an educator, personal growth knows no bounds. Therefore, an underlying philosophy for shaping judicious consequences must be carefully weighed and practiced until, like second nature, it becomes spontaneous.

Very important to effective communication is that both parties believe they have some control in the conversation. While working toward an equitable solution, students must believe their feelings and opinions are a valued part of the process.

The secret to shaping consequences, therefore, is to work with students on solutions that are **volitional** on their part—a process in which they feel **they** have made the decision and that **they** "have made something right again" when it is carried out. In the long run, this sense of accountability feels much better to students than being "let off the hook" with a lecture from an authority figure.

A good example comes from an elementary principal who recently told me about an encounter she had with one of her students. Sitting together in her office, they had just worked out an agreement as a solution to a problem the student had in school. As he was leaving her office, she asked him "you're not going to have any trouble carrying out your part of the bargain, are you?" The student turned to her with a look of disbelief and said: "Why would I? It's my agreement, isn't it?"

Exemplifying the intended behavior is also an effective strategy for empowering students, meaning that educators should not hesitate to join in and help students having trouble. Modeling problem solving is far from a picture of vulnerability or even of indulgence, instead it is a demonstration of strength, cooperation, and leadership qualities. It also provides an excellent opportunity to do things **with** students instead of doing things **to** them. Educators who view mistakes as an opportunity to demonstrate how to recover and treat others experiencing misfortune are emulated often and long remembered.

An example comes to mind of a high school experience related by a student in the Educational Psychology class I teach. He and several others wanted to test their school's new vice principal by throwing rolls of toilet paper over and around his house one evening near the beginning of the school year.

The next day, they were all called into his office, but instead of the usual lecture and suspension they were expecting, the vice-principal asked the students if they would come over after school and help him clean up the mess. The surprised students arrived at his house to find that he had ladders and rakes ready for them. But they were really shocked when the vice principal himself proceeded to help them clean up the mess they had made. His wife brought them soft drinks and at dinner time she prepared hamburgers for everyone.

The student told us that because of the way he handled this incident the new vice principal immediately gained great respect from students and faculty alike. That single experience, he confessed to the class, had such an impact on his behavior that he changed from being a troublemaker to someone who really cared about helping the school become a better place.

Educators should avoid shaping consequences before behav-

123

ioral problems occur. For example, a teacher who threatened "if you do that one more time I will send you to the office" would be setting in motion a possible action from which it would be hard to retreat.

Teachers who do this often box themselves into a poor decision. Another problem with predetermined consequences is that students often play games with threatened "cut-and-dried" consequences. For example, knowing that the third infraction means being sent to the office almost invites two disruptions by a troublesome student.

When narrow lines are drawn, students seem to want to stand on them or jump back and forth over them. However, educators who are patient and confident in their professional abilities draw broad lines students must walk across. This gives them time to diagnose the problem and help students change their attitude before they reach the other side.

Individualizing Consequences

There are two important aspects in determining consequences for each student's misbehavior. The first is to understand the real nature of the problem, and the second is to account for individual differences among students.

For example, if two culpable students were asked to clean up a vandalized wall and one student replies "OK, I have the time right after school" and the other belligerently responds "that's not my job, that's janitor's work and you can't make me do it" the underlying problem is different for the two students. As a result, a different approach and consequence would be needed to get to the heart of each student's individual differences.

In the case of the first student, the wall would be cleaned

willingly, and in all likelihood would not be perceived as punishment but rather as a reasonable act of recovery from someone ready to make amends and get it over with right away.

As for the other student, a more serious problem has surfaced, and scrubbing the wall now becomes secondary to getting to the cause of a defiant attitude that is now apparent as the underlying problem.

This is exactly the time troublesome students need guidance and individual attention if they are going to stay in school. It is also precisely the moment an educator needs to keep personal feelings of anger and frustration under control.

The use of effective communication and problem solving skills become the important next steps as the true nature of the difficulty presents itself. Workable resolutions will emerge as students temper their anger and have an opportunity to express their side of the story in the problem solving process.

This mutual process of working towards a resolution often requires time for student attitudes to change. When this change does happen, however, it may be too late for the second student to help clean the wall. But with a change in attitude, it is likely the second student could decide to rectify his or her past indiscretion by participating in clean-up activities at school as well as apologizing and thanking those who did clean it up.

On the other hand, if both students feel they were forced to do the cleaning, the first student who did not need to be coerced could resent it as punishment, and the second student's indignant attitude would not only go unattended, but could lead to bitter reprisal and an escalation of the problem.

A major concern often expressed when individualizing consequences is the fear that students will fault educators for being unfair if students are treated differently from one another. However, this is true only for educators who use punishment. These educators are forced to punish consistently as students are usually quick to remind them of classmates who were punished differently for committing exactly the same offense.

But consequences should not be designed to punish students. By definition, Judicious Consequences are designed to take into account individual differences among students in order to meet the emotional and learning needs of each person involved. Being educational in nature, students who misbehave simply may have different ways of learning from their mistakes, and, as a result, different consequences are necessary.

For example, two students experiencing difficulty reading would not necessarily both improve their reading if given the same learning strategies by their teacher; they may likely react differently to that or any other single learning strategy. It only makes sense, then, for educators to employ different educational consequences as they work with the many different individual needs and attitudes students bring to behavioral problems.

Although a mentoring approach to behavioral problems is sound professional practice, unknowing students are going to question the inconsistency of educators' actions. It is important, therefore, to respond to these inquiries in a professional manner, without revealing the confidentiality of the matter. Getting back to the scenario, for example, an educator's response to the student who did clean the wall might sound something like: "I have determined from the other student's response that there are some other problems we are going to have to discuss. We are going to be working this out and it will be handled in another way." The student who did clean up the wall will know the consequences designed to change an attitude are only beginning with the other student and that they are both in the hands of a capable professional.

When students perceive their consequences as educational in nature, feel they make sense for them, and are allowed to act on their own volition, they may show little interest in comparing what they are learning from their misbehavior to that which others may need to learn.

Timing is very important to sustain good communication between students and teachers. For example, educators should make every attempt to respond to problems as soon as possible, to avoid the discomforting ambiguity that accompanies students' misbehavior. A quick response not only spares students the mental anguish of something being held over their heads, but allows them to experience some immediate control and responsibility for rectifying the situation. There is also something cleansing about getting past unpleasant experiences quickly and putting things back on track again. This is also equally true for educators; both parties are usually relieved when a difficult episode is over.

Another problem common to schools is **fighting**. Individualizing consequences in such cases is always a difficult challenge, because it is so widely accepted by educators that regardless of the circumstances, both parties to a fight are to be summarily suspended from school. The traditional thinking is both that suspension is a show of force to students and faculty, demonstrating that something is being done, and also that the threat of suspension will deter fighting. As a result, educators who choose to work with the causes of the fight and who wish to get the two combatants to peaceably express their differences are often perceived as "too soft."

But from the students' viewpoint, the safest place to fight may be at school. As they move through their "rites of passage," many students are so caught up in the peer pressure that they must occasionally show they are unafraid to stand their ground. Many of these students are reluctant to fight. But if they are faced with fighting, they prefer to do it at school. Not only will others be around to witness their act of courage, but they are hopeful that someone will stop the fight if goes too far. The same fight off school grounds does not have the same safeguards and can quickly get out of hand. As a result, school rules against fighting have little effect on adolescents trying to "save face" as well as

127

trying not to get beaten up too badly.

Because venue is one of the primary issues of students fighting, it cannot be ignored in developing judicious consequences. If educators are going to develop a workable approach to fighting at school, they must take into consideration the reality of students' dilemmas. And just as important, educators must find ways to deal with the outside pressure that they "better be doing something about the fighting problem." The label of "too soft", therefore, must somehow be replaced with a forceful message to the school community that there is a professional commitment to keep students in school.

This does not mean condoning student fights, but it does recognize that an automatic suspension will not eliminate fighting. It does not mean taking no action with students who were fighting, but it does mean doing everything possible to keep them in their regular classrooms.

As with other student behavior problems, fighting can be approached as a manifestation of a personal problem between students who need professional assistance. If counseling, mentoring, and mediation resources are available and consistently carried out, students, faculty, and the community will be fully aware that "something positive is being done" about fighting at school, and at the same time the students involved have not missed valuable classroom activities.

For example, peer mediation programs are very effective alternatives to suspension. These models employ social skills training in the areas of listening, problem solving, and mediation using peers as mediators for conflict between students. The underlying theory in these programs is that once students have the ability to resolve conflicts among themselves, they have a sense of control in social situations. These programs have proved very successful in cutting down the number of student confrontations as well as keeping students in school.

The year Garfield Elementary School in Mankato, Minnesota, a sixth grade-only school, adopted ***Judicious Discipline***, there was not a single fight at school. The principal, Bob Moss, told me that when students learn the language of civility, they will use it to resolve their disputes instead of fighting. A good example that knowledge is power.

Another good example of something positive was told to me by a student in my Educational Psychology class who related his own experience with fighting in school. During his first three years of high school, he and another student had been suspended numerous times for fighting with each other. His senior year, the school hired a new assistant principal who, after yet another fight, called them both into his office. He got them talking about their feelings toward each other and reminiscing about the reasons for their history of fighting. He walked with them down to the cafeteria, where the three of them had lunch together. Not only did they never fight again, but they graduated from high school as best friends.

This student recalled that the threat of suspension was simply not a deterrent to the two of them fighting. Not until the new assistant principal took the time and made the effort to help them work through their problems with each other would pride let either of them change their attitude and behavior. If students perceive school as a safe place where they can grow and develop under the mentorship of capable professionals, they will be far less likely to abuse the system; and they will be cooperative with those making every effort to help them.

Some educators argue, however, that judicious consequences are not tough enough and therefore will not deter students from misbehaving. Many feel that in the "heat of the battle" hearing students out and working through problems seems to be an undue burden for which there is too little time. In the short run, there may be some validity to these arguments.

But when that window of opportunity presents itself, educators can little afford **not** to take the time necessary to help each student progress and grow from their misconduct. In the long run, educators spend much more time scolding, reminding, coaxing, confronting, demanding, lecturing, lamenting, conjecturing, and cajoling, than they ever would taking the time and effort needed to develop attitudes of respect and responsibility that will last students a lifetime.

In summary, I have often wondered why some students seem to enjoy finding out what they can get away with, but others behave in an entirely different manner. I have come to the conclusion that students find no fun at all trying to disrupt learning environments in which they perceive their educators are making every effort to empower them, treat them as significant, and allow them to gain confidence in their ability to handle their own affairs.

CHAPTER 6:
BALANCING
RIGHTS
AND RESPONSIBILITIES

The purpose of this chapter is to provide a resource from which educators can draw as they apply the principles of *Judicious Discipline*. It is the synthesis of constitutional rights, good educational practice, and professional ethics counterbalanced with the everyday realities of student discipline and achievement. This chapter is not meant to be all inclusive of disciplinary and educational issues facing educators, but it does contain many representative examples of school practices that affect student rights and responsibilities.

Whereas Chapter 3 presents a constitutional framework that is well established and has served our nation for two hundred years, this chapter on applying students' rights in public schools is constantly changing. The dynamics of balancing students' rights require educators to stay abreast of new laws and good educational practices. As laws are promulgated and awareness of discriminatory practices increases, educators must change accordingly as they seek to model for students exemplary standards of tolerance and educational leadership. All too often it is an uninformed and insensitive educator who serves as the lifeblood of an uninviting and confrontive school environment.

As educators search for ways to create an environment that provides an equal educational opportunity for all students, they must keep in mind the scales of justice and the loneliness of one student looking across at all the other students. Although some of the subject matter examined may appear to have little to do with discipline and achievement, the subtle nature of violating human rights cuts deep into feelings of self-worth and is often the cause for placing students at risk. Chapter 6 is designed to provide educators a judicious and consistent rationale for creating a learning environment that provides freedom, justice, and equality for all.

Compulsory School Attendance

Legitimate educational purpose is the state's compelling interest to require children to attend school. The government denies children's liberty by forcing upon them an education designed to make them self-sufficient as adults so that they will not become a burden on society. An enlightened citizenry also leads to a safer and more powerful nation. Although there are exceptions to these laws, home schooling for example, they nonetheless infringe on the liberty of children and their families. Because of this intrusion into the arena of family traditions, educators must respect individual family values while enforcing the welfare needs of the state.

Too many schools attempt to intimidate students by citing state law at the beginning of their attendance policies, followed by a long list of punishing consequences for non-attendance. Many students perceive this as a threat that "you better come to school or we will kick you out." As uninviting and incongruent as these rules are, their primary purpose is to keep desirable students in and undesirables out, often resulting in a push-out phenomenon. Attendance policies either serve as society's gates to educational opportunities or function as the walls of despair for students at risk.

If educators decide their professional responsibility is to teach and serve students who exhibit behavior problems, academic deficiencies, bad attitudes, or whose cultural values may be offensive, the gate will be open and a commitment to help all students will be mirrored in the attendance policy. If the opposite attitude is practiced, then the walls will be put in place to bar students perceived as being less worthy of the benefits of public schooling.

State compulsory education laws are relatively easy to follow and carry out when educators use them to coerce children to school, and at the same time to deny education to those who skip school or misbehave. It is much harder, however, for educators to view these same state laws as an opportunity for all children to receive an education and then apply the same laws to keep students in school rather than pushing them out. This philosophical difference with which educators approach school attendance is pivotal to creating a learning environment that is inviting to students as well as committed to helping them stay in the learning community.

As necessary as compulsory attendance laws are to establish expectations for students, they are often the cause of antithetical situations for educators. A case in point are state laws that mandate a specific number of **days required to attend** high school in order to graduate. When strictly enforced, the attendance requirement may not appear to be reasonably connected to its original intent.

For example, a high school senior with a combined SAT score of 1250 who is absent more than the permissible number of days has a good argument that the attendance requirement should not

133

prevent graduation. The question is whether to allow the student to graduate or require the student to return the following fall term to make up for seat-time missed. Although graduating a non-attending student may violate the letter of the law, a 1250 SAT score suggests the student has met the spirit of the law's intent. Therefore, rules pertaining to the number of school days required for graduation should be used as guidelines and enforcement should be based on the facts relevant to each individual case.

Another issue related to attendance is **credit denial** and/or **dropping students** after a specified number of absences. The rationale for these rules is usually to deter students from missing too much school. However, many schools are finding students playing games with such rules by purposely missing school up to one day short of the specified days.

Schools must legally include an appeal process for students who are dropped but want to return during the same grading period. At question in the appeal is not the validity of the rule, but rather the individual circumstances that serve as the substance of the appeal. Administrators need to consider each individual case carefully and base decisions on whether or not the student is able to complete the course work satisfactorily during that grading period. If students can show an ability to complete the work adequately without causing an undue hardship for the teacher, permission should be granted to complete the required work regardless of the motive behind the absences.

If decisions allowing students to return are based on their reasons for non-attendance, all too often they will lead administrators into a quagmire of family values. Educators should decide the issue of readmission based on sound educational practices and avoid moral judgments. For example, students who skip school and students who are ill both come back with the same educational problem. They both need to make up the coursework missed if they are to succeed in school. There is no need to treat them differently if they both can demonstrate they are capable of making up the missed classes.

Another common problem is the quandary students, parents, and educators face over **excused and unexcused absences**. Take, for instance, two students who skip school all day to play video games together at a local convenience store. One parent is willing to write an excused absence and the other parent is not. Although they were together during the absence, the students may experience very different consequences when they return to school. The excused student is usually given reasonable help to complete the school work missed and the other will probably be punished with a short suspension and not be allowed to make up missed tests and assignments.

Excused and unexcused absences also bring up several contradictory and ethical questions. Schools often place parents in the dilemma of choosing between lying to keep their children from experiencing a serious setback to their education or modeling for their children the value of honesty. If attendance is important to success in school, then professional educators are not acting in the best interests of students when they exacerbate learning problems by pushing students away from valued learning opportunities. In addition to all of this, educators cannot ignore the irony of punishing students with exactly what the rules forbid—absence from school—and not allowing them to make up their missed schoolwork.

These contradictions send a powerful message that school officials do not trust students or parents to make educationally and morally sound decisions. Due to this mistrust, educators often find themselves appearing righteous and moralistic as they battle with students and parents over the value of a family vacation or the need for a student to care for an ill sibling so that the parents can go to work. Also, there are occasionally questionable excused absences for "the chosen few," causing educators to appear unreasonable. For example, students excused to decorate

135

the gym for a carnival, run errands for teachers, or participate in sports may miss more class time than those who are caught skipping school.

Administrators can easily avoid these antithetical situations by not distinguishing between excused and unexcused absences and simply recording student absences. If a student without a prearranged absence is not in attendance, the school should contact the parents or guardians to inform them of this fact. School officials should trust parents and guardians by placing attendance issues in their hands, while cooperating fully with resources available at school. At school, educators should not treat the matter so much as a behavioral question, but rather as an issue of academic success in school. It makes it easier for everyone if the consequence of being absent is for students to answer to their parents for their absence, and to their teachers for the academic work missed.

Another consideration is the issue of **school curriculum**. Many parents today are requesting a review of school activities and curriculum materials that may be in conflict with their family values. The frequently questioned activities include areas such as values clarification, evolution, sex and death education, drugs, globalism, psychological/attitudinal testing, and subject matter described as secular humanism. The Hatch Amendment of 1978 is cited as the legal basis for these requests. It allows parents to inspect all instructional materials designed to explore "new and unproven" teaching techniques.

The Amendment, however, applies only to programs that are funded through the United States Department of Education and not to programs funded through other federal agencies or state or local sources. Although this federal law affects only a small part of a school's curriculum, the spirit of openness and reasonable exceptions of this law provide an opportunity for educators to encourage parental participation in the education of their children. When parents reasonably disagree with curriculum requirements, educators should make every effort to excuse their children from part or all of the course in question.

By encouraging parents and guardians to take an active role in decisions that impact their family traditions, the educational and disciplinary problems with students are significantly lessened. Rules and decisions not supported by parents have little effect on students who feel they have license from home to disrupt in ways that mirror their family values. Not only are educators directing time away from academics in favor of disruptive students, but additional time and effort is spent on unnecessary parent conferences. For parents who become disillusioned or find themselves at odds with public schools, there is always the option of private schools or home schooling.

Tardiness is difficult to manage with any degree of consistency because of problems associated with its definition. In one class, being tardy means arriving one second after the bell, while in another it may mean arriving five minutes late, depending on the management style of the teachers in question. The attempts of most administrators at imposing some sort of consistency among faculty typically end in futility. As a result, in an effort to be consistent, they employ a strict rules-and-punishment approach to alleviate the problem.

Rules used in most schools require that tardy students be sent to the office for an excuse, that after a warning or two they report for detention, and that after several more they may receive a short suspension. This punishment approach often leads to other educational and administrative problems, such as time allocated to students obtaining excuses, class disruption when students reenter with their excuses, students playing games with the rule by deliberately being late twice but not the critical third time, difficulty in judging or proving excuses, and finally the problems associated with an emphasis on obedience rather than learning personal responsibility.

Therefore, rules and consequences for tardiness should at-

137

tempt to mitigate educational disruptions as well as teach and encourage the value of being on time. For this reason, teachers are in the best position to regulate tardiness and should be given the authority to resolve their own problems.

The first day of class could include a discussion about why it is important for students and teachers to be in class on time, why people are most often late, and what kinds of disruptions latecomers cause. The class could work together to decide the appropriate manner for students to enter the classroom without disturbing the learning environment. If the office needs to know who is absent and who is tardy, the tardy students could assume the responsibility of that notification.

Students who are tardy can be asked to remain after class to discuss the reasons. If the reasons make sense to the teacher, the matter is closed. If not, both can work on a mutually agreeable plan. If the problem turns out to be one of attitude, tardiness is only the symptom and educators should then change their focus away from the infraction towards a discussion of the student's feelings about the class and the importance of punctuality. When personal problems are at issue, it may be necessary to recruit the help of counselors or other educators who have a good working rapport with the student. Administrators should become involved only with chronic problems or when teachers have exhausted their own resources.

One of the best strategies to discourage tardiness is for teachers to start class on time. A well-prepared, ready-to-go teacher, modeling behavior congruent with expectations, sends a powerful message to lingering students. It also follows that when teachers are late, an immediate apology and short explanation to the class is in order.

Educators must approach tardiness as a means to build community rather than view it as a game or foul play in need of punishment. As with all other behavioral problems, the principal issues when discussing tardiness are trust and mutual respect between teachers and students. Students can immediately sense the difference between teachers using fear of punishment to control promptness from those who want to help students learn to feel responsible for being on time for class.

Suspension is a short-term denial of the student's right to an education. This may range from very short in-house suspensions to removal from school for a period from seven up to thirty days, depending on various state laws. Because the absence is brief, a student usually suffers no substantial loss of educational opportunities. For this reason, the law accords students mostly procedural due process rights. These procedural rights were set out in *Goss v. Lopez*, 419 U.S. 565, and require the school administrator to provide at least:

1. **Notice**—an oral or written notice of the charges; i.e., the rule the student violated.
2. **Evidence**—a summary of the evidence against the student; i.e., a teacher witnessed the student's misbehavior.
3. **Defense**—an opportunity for the student to be heard; i.e., the student has an opportunity to tell his or her side of the story.

If the student demands an attorney or presentation of witnesses, an administrator may choose not to comply with the student's demands unless local law holds otherwise. The Court balanced a student's right to procedural due process against the school's need not to be overburdened with time consuming student hearings. Because there is a time limit on suspensions, suspending students until their parents come to school for a conference may in some cases violate students' due process rights.

The concept of In-school Suspensions should be changed to something like Educational Opportunities Center, where there is an emphasis on continued learning activities. Avoiding the word "suspension" alleviates the stigma associated with punishment and being excluded from a learning environment. Changing the designation also is a good first step in moving students from a negative experience of feeling incarcerated to a positive one of feeling the school wants to help them academically somewhere else in the building. This concept will work best if students experiencing a bad day can choose for themselves this alternative for learning in lieu of remaining in their regular classrooms. In other words, "Where would you like to learn today, back in your classroom or in the Educational Opportunities Center?"

As educationally sound as in-school suspensions appear, the most equal educational opportunity for students is in their regular classroom environment. In cases where students become a threat to the safety of the school community, they may have to be suspended until their threatening behavior changes. When this happens, administrative style is often pivotal to influencing the student's attitude when he or she returns to school.

For example, if suspension is meted out as punishment ("this will teach you a lesson"), an adversarial relationship usually develops. But if suspension is viewed as a chance to get away from school and cool down a bit ("we could both use time away from each other"), a professional relationship remains solid. The second also implies that considerable effort was made to help the student stay in school, but a resolution of the problem could not been reached.

In addition, administrators should communicate the school's interest in the student's continued welfare by providing students with academic assignments and offering them after-school and/or week-end tutoring. An act of friendship would be to walk students to the bicycle rack or to the parking lot and even call them during their suspension to wish them well and indicate that the school is looking forward to their return.

Being excluded from the school community, even for a short

time, is painful for students; educators who remain professional friends to such students do much to alleviate the loneliness and bitterness associated with the separation. An administrative style that is sensitive to the self-esteem needs of students, as well as the concerns of the student's family during a suspension, fosters a positive attitude toward school by keeping intact the all-important student/educator relationship.

Although courts have dealt only with suspensions from school, fair and consistent building policy would require the same procedural due process steps be taken by teachers who consider the removal of students from their classrooms. If teachers would take the time to explain the problem and hear the student's side of a story, a better decision than having the student leave the classroom might be made. When the teacher's decision is to send the student to the office, the request to the administration should be for their help in keeping the student in school and getting him or her back in the regular classroom as soon as possible.

Expulsions are for a longer duration than suspensions, and usually result in the loss of grades, credits, and a substantial deprivation of educational opportunities. For this reason, students faced with expulsion have both substantive and procedural due process rights. Not only must schools provide the charges, evidence, and a hearing, but they must also substantiate the reasons for expulsion. In addition, students have a right to be represented by counsel, review all records, bring witnesses, cross examine, receive a complete and accurate record of the proceedings, and appeal the decision.

As with suspensions, educators should make every effort to communicate the school's interest in the student's welfare, including advice and help in locating alternative educational opportunities. Because an expulsion is the "final blow" and the worst possible action school districts can inflict on students, a nonconfrontive style during the separation is very important if the student/educator relationship is to remain viable.

141

One approach would be, instead of blaming students for the problems leading to the expulsion, to talk to them and their parents about the resources that were not available in order to keep them in school. A statement such as: "We have tried a lot of things hoping to make this work, but we have simply run out of resources. We simply do not have the personnel capable of dealing with your problem. I am sorry we have failed, but we are going to have to spend some time away from each other. When you feel you can work with the resources we have at school, we will be happy to have you come back."

By separating the student from the problems that available resources cannot resolve, it leaves students feeling that they are valued and are left with power in the consequence to choose when to come back. When someone asks why they are not in school, there is a big difference between students saying "I've been kicked out" and a response like "the school ran out of resources so we've separated for a while."

Students with disabilities have additional rights to educational opportunities that do not flow to regular students. Because a student's disability may be cause for a suspension or expulsion, federal and state laws require other procedures that must be followed. To stay informed of the changing law in the field of special education, educators should seek advice from knowledgeable special educators and legal counsel in matters pertaining to both suspensions and expulsions of students with disabilities.

Grading Practices

Liberty Interests

The letter grade on a report card or transcript is generally perceived as the student's level of skill and understanding of the subject matter. Because past academic achievement and the skills they represent are critical to predicting success, students' grades are used often by educators and employers as a basis for deciding future opportunities. However, due to the excessive entanglement between **achievement** and **behavior**, achievement grades are often misinterpreted.

For example, an academically gifted student whose grade is lowered because of absences, late papers, or a bad attitude in class could likely be misassigned the next year or even be deprived of future employment or schooling opportunities. As a result, educators' grading practices may be putting in jeopardy students' Fourteenth Amendment right of liberty.

Notwithstanding the authority teachers have to determine curriculum and standards for grades, a student's future opportunities must not hinge on what the teacher thinks the grade means, but what the widespread consensus of those who interpret the grade think it means. For example, lowering a grade for a late assignment in a creative writing course would be different from lowering a grade for missing a deadline in a journalism class. Whereas learning punctuality in order to meet press time could be an expected achievement in the field of journalism for a grade in a journalism class, it would not be considered as a measure of achievement for those interpreting a grade in a class on creative writing.

143

Therefore, it is important to incorporate in the academic grade only those requirements and standards commonly understood by "the profession" or the community at large to be course content. A plausible test would be to ask parents, employers, other faculty members, and experts in the field what they believe an "A" or a "C" means in specific classes. The liberty issue lies not in what the grade means to the teacher or the student, but that it **communicates to the reader** an accurate statement of the student's academic achievement.

Although behavioral information is very important to those deciding on the future opportunities of students, it should be passed on separately through other means. The most effective form of disclosing behavioral information is through discourse, where questions and clarification between interested parties allow them the best chance to flesh out relevant and pertinent information. A distant second best would be written statements describing facts and events about student behavior directly related to the matter in question. Letter grades and check-lists simply allow for no give-and-take, which opens up even more the possibility of miscommunication. For example, how much can a "U" in citizenship on a student's report card communicate to an interested parent or guardian?

Educators often cite "real world" reasons to lower grades, for such things as tardiness, poor attitude, or late assignments. They argue that these and other similar behavior patterns can often lead to being fired from jobs and that having students experience this lesson in school will prove beneficial to them later on when they enter the workplace. How many times have teachers said in this context "you will thank me some day for this." However, many of these students who are continually late in school are never late for their job after school. Lowering achievement grades for misbehavior does not always teach responsibility, but it always does pass on misinformation.

Students in school are still **learning** promptness and a

cooperative attitude. They should not be experiencing an employer/employee relationship with their teacher; indeed, in the workplace such relationships are often adversarial. Instead, students should be experiencing a professional relationship with their teacher/mentors, who are using educational strategies designed to develop and change attitudes. Furthermore, students in public schools have liberty rights, but employees in the private sector do not.

Employers have discovered it is not good business to fire someone they have spent time and money to hire and train, only to have to go through the process again with someone else. They have also learned that employees' productivity and attendance are not related as much to fear of dismissal as to the positive aspects of personal accomplishment and pride in the product or service.

The law today requires management in business and manufacturing to help workers who are experiencing problems in the workplace by offering them assistance, such as counseling, rehabilitation, retraining, and educational help. Until employers have, in good faith, tried to help a troubled employee succeed on the job, they cannot legally dismiss them. If this educational approach is good for business, then the concepts of judicious grading practices are very much in line with the "real world" of business and industry.

Late Assignments

The approach teachers use to handle late assignments reveals immediately whether or not they are student-centered. By accepting and not grading down late work, educators send a professional message to students that completing assignments, receiving teachers feedback, and being fairly evaluated are all important to their educational success.

Conversely, educators who do not accept or who grade down late assignments generally have two reasons. They argue: (1) administrative convenience—that unless penalized most students will hand in all their work at the end of the grading period, not leaving the teacher adequate time for grading; and (2) teaching responsibility—that students should learn to be responsible for getting work done on time because this is what is going to happen to them in the real world.

These contradicting philosophies were a source of frustration to a former graduate student who returned to visit with me several years after completing her degree. As an experienced English teacher, she had always reasoned that with many papers to grade, a strategy was needed to pressure students to complete their work on time; she feared the alternative would be a deluge of papers at the end of each grading period. Even though she continued her policy, she always had the feeling that there was something not fair about lowering grades on well-written papers. When she re-examined the issue in light of student liberty interests, she knew she had to find another approach. After trying several alternatives that did not work, she finally settled on the following plan.

She begins her class with a review of the course requirements, one of which is a short composition due every two weeks. She continues with an explanation that these assignments will be evaluated and returned within a few days. She expands on the educational value of writing practice, learning from mistakes, and the benefits of her feedback. In addition, she informs the class that she has over one hundred fifty students a week and has budgeted just enough time to correct and return papers handed in on schedule. She emphasizes that it is to their educational advantage and her administrative convenience for compositions to be submitted on a regular basis.

Next, she points to two boxes on her desk; one labeled "papers on time" and the other "late papers." She informs her students that papers coming in on time will be corrected and returned as promised; late compositions will be processed and returned as time allows, or possibly sometime next term. If she cannot get to them, students can expect an "incomplete" in the course until she can read the papers.

In other words, late papers...late grades. She smiled when she told me she now has very few problems with late papers. No longer does she constantly have to remind students of deadlines or grade down good writing, and, as a result, more of her students are doing their work and accepting the responsibility for turning in their work on time. As a footnote, some teachers using this two-box system have added a third box for "early papers." They report that some students really like the early box and that it also provides an opportunity to get a head start on the papers.

Late assignments are something teachers can quickly turn into positive learning experiences for students as well as themselves. Inquiry may result in teachers finding that students do not have the skills to do the assignment, or their personal life is such that it just could not get done. Some students have little experience meeting deadlines and really need help learning how to organize their time and to set goals for themselves. By turning late assignments into learning experiences, teachers move immediately from the role of enforcer to that of educator.

Teachers who accept late work tell me that students are more likely to complete their assignments if they know it will not be graded down, thereby learning and benefiting more from the coursework. It also communicates to students that all class assignments have a legitimate educational purpose that must be fulfilled. Many educators are also discussing due dates for assignments with students based on how much time they feel the student will need to complete the work. Taking into account the students' needs and interests gives them some ownership in the deadline.

But there are those who argue that accepting late assign-

147

ments is unfair to other students, because more time has been allowed to complete the assignment. However, if all students are allowed the same chance to hand in late assignments, then all will have the same equal opportunity to give the assignment their best effort. Some teachers fear students will take advantage of this approach and hand in all assignments late. Many educators believe only problems will result from placing so much responsibility in the hands of their students. Almost all who try this method of accepting late work, however, discover their fears to be unfounded. Instead, most experience a sense of professional pride in the fact that their students are now completing their assignments without all the prodding and loss of interest associated with late work penalties.

There is something antithetical about an educational assignment that, when late, is not accepted by a "professional educator." The assignment was made in the best interests of the student's educational success, and if not accepted, the student's interests are simply not being served. Students suddenly get the feeling their teacher does not really care about their success in class and has simply given up on them. The message being sent to students is that being punctual is far more important than the educational value of the coursework assigned.

While an early/on-time/late box solution may not work for every teacher, it is one example of how to handle late assignments in a way consistent with goals of fostering academic ability and achievement. In addition, it creates an environment in which students experience personal accountability while at the same time it models the professional responsibility of teachers.

The Incomplete Grade

Administrators who allow and encourage teachers the judicious use of the "incomplete" grade offer their teachers an opportunity to be fair and accurate in their grading practices. This option does not have the effect of diminishing class rigor, and sends a message to students that until all assignments and tests are complete, they will not receive a grade or credit for the class. Prudent administrative policy would allow a reasonable time for students to make up required work. This "reasonable time" could vary depending on the student's need for course credit or the availability of the teacher involved.

If course work is not completed within a reasonable time frame, the "I" should remain an "I" or be changed to a "NG" (no grade) or a "W" (withdraw). However, changing an "I" to an "F" would imply the student did complete the course work, but failed to understand the subject matter or meet the course standards, thus sending an incorrect message.

An "I," "NG," or "W," on the other hand, would not misinform the person interpreting the transcript and would simply mean the student did not complete the course. The "I," however, could have a beneficial effect on marginal students. The difference between telling students that they did not finish the course or that they failed could be the difference between deciding to continue in school or not.

In the event an "I" needs to be changed to an achievement grade, such as for graduation purposes, a grade could be compiled from the information available. If in the professional judgment of the teacher there is enough evidence to determine the student's mastery of the subject, the grade could be negotiated with the student at that time. Whether the student receives a grade and credit should always remain the professional judgment of the student's teacher based upon reasonable course expectations.

Elementary and middle schools have an excellent opportunity to be flexible and innovative when reporting student behavior and achievement. Unlike high schools, they are not limited to the letter grade system expected by employers and college admission offices. Although many parents demand some sort of letter grade,

149

usually for comparison purposes, there is still an opportunity to elaborate on an incomplete, missed assignments, the tests not taken, the number of late arrivals, absences, and other behavioral information.

Many elementary teachers use a system of portfolio assessment that incorporates student input into the grading process and results in narratives describing student achievement in a variety of areas. Parents of elementary students are more likely to attend conferences to receive firsthand behavioral information and are usually more responsive to suggested ideas for learning activities at home. Instead of trying to use one letter to tell the whole story, elementary and middle school teachers should be using a descriptive and narrative reporting system that presents a complete and accurate picture of student achievement and development.

Other Behavioral Issues in Grading Achievement

It is sometimes very difficult to separate **student attitudes** from achievement grades. Most educators will agree that it is easier to grade fairly students with good attitudes who are always on task and in their seats than it is to remain objective when assessing less attentive or rebellious students. When educators' insecurities concerning their expertise or authority get bruised, the tendency is to want to retaliate against students by grading them more harshly.

However, objectivity and fairness in grading are very important to student liberty interests. Although it is sometimes very difficult, educators must somehow get beyond the fact they have been hurt by a student's poor attitude. This really takes practice with some students. But by not thinking about previous behavior and focusing intently on helping all students succeed academically, it can become a well-earned intrinsic reward.

It is common practice for students caught **cheating** on exams or **plagiarizing** assignments to receive an "F" for their work. This is normally averaged with their other grades or used as the final grade in the course. The problem with this practice is that an "F" connotes academic achievement (or lack of it) and will be interpreted as such by those who read it. Because cheating and plagiarism are behavioral issues, rather than academic indices, they should be treated separately.

This is an excellent opportunity to work with students on the problems that lead up to the act of cheating or plagiarizing itself. For example, a student caught cheating on an exam could be offered a make-up exam, possibly the same one given to students who did not take the test due to illness. By the same token, plagiarizing should entail completing another paper or report covering the same topic. Educators must separate fair and accurate evaluation from their professional responsibilities aimed at getting to the real issues of student misbehavior.

In addition to providing for alternative academic evaluations and requirements, students should be on notice from the first class meeting that cheating and plagiarizing are serious behavioral matters. It is important for students to know from the beginning that exemplary as well as deceitful conduct will have an effect on how others will evaluate them. In some instances their future opportunities in school and life may be at stake. Although achievement grades will not be affected, there will be conferences about the problem and consequences designed to resolve the issue. Educators will not only be much more effective in holding together the professional student/educator relationship, but will be protecting student liberties in the difficult arena of cheating and plagiarizing.

Whether to use **norm-referenced** or **criterion-referenced grading** reflects the teaching philosophy of every educator. In norm-referenced grading, the other students in the class provide the norms for determining the meaning of a given individual's grade. This is sometimes refered to as "grading on the curve," where there is only a limited number of each grade awarded. Teachers using this type of competitive grading do not provide an equal educational opportunity for all students to be graded on what they have achieved in the course.

Criterion-referenced grading, on the other hand, is when achievement is not compared to that of others, but rather to a given criterion or standard of performance. This is a student-centered grading philosophy and allows everyone an equal opportunity to pass specific course standards. In theory, all students could receive a high grade if they in fact achieved the relevant course criterion. Although all students seldom receive the highest grade, this grading practice is by definition encouraging to students and gives them the message that their teacher is truly working in **each** of their best interests.

Class attendance is often commingled with the academic grade. Every educator knows when students miss class they lose the benefits of learning that occur in the normal course of classroom activities. But instead of grading down for non-attendance, educational alternatives should be developed and required that are closely related to the classroom discussions and activities missed during students' absences. It is common for teachers to prepare learning assignments for students going on a pre-arranged family vacation or for students absent due to an extended illness. The same approach could be used as educational alternatives for those who have been absent.

Other examples of educational alternatives for absent students might be doing the coursework collaboratively with parents at home or a tutor after school, writing a short paper covering the subject matter discussed, a book or chapter review on the subject, or several pages outlining the missed chapters discussed in class. To alleviate the overload generated by educational alternatives and make-up work, schools should provide volunteer tutors and schedule times during the school day, evenings, or week-ends when help would be available. Well-planned alternative assignments not only offer students their right to an equal education, but emphasize the importance of class rigor and academic expectations.

In the event that alternative assignments are viewed by some students as punishment for being absent, a clear explanation would be necessary to illustrate that it is an educational expectation in lieu of what other students learned in class. The difference could be that students considering whether or not to skip class might think "do I want to learn the course material in class, **or**, do I want to learn the course material doing an alternative assignment?"

I was confronted at a workshop by a teacher who asked "are you telling me that if a student has been ill and another was skipping, that they should both be able to make up the work missed?" My response was that both needed an educator when they returned, perhaps the one who skipped more than the other. Regardless of the reason for the students' absences, make up work and late assignments should be accepted to ensure those students an equal educational opportunity.

Excused and unexcused absences are not relevant to an achievement grade. There is no legitimate educational purpose for distinguishing between excused and unexcused absences. For educational purposes, therefore, there only needs to be recorded absences. Those absent, for whatever reason, would simply make up the missed class experience with alternative learning assignments or other mutually agreed upon learning activities.

This approach avoids the difficulty educators face when trying to decide whether a student is actually ill or that there was in fact an emergency situation that kept the them from attending class. Checking the validity of excuses is at best unmanageable and often leads to an adversarial confrontation over the veracity of the student's word.

Students are unfortunately conditioned over the years to

153

plead and sometimes lie as they explain absences or request exceptions. I am always amazed by the relief on their faces when I interrupt my students in the middle of their unsolicited excuse by saying: "I respect the decision you have made not to be in class. You may tell me if you wish, but we also need to talk about other ways for you to cover what the rest of us went over in class." Invariably their attitude becomes one of cooperation and interest in what they had missed.

Class participation is often used as a criterion because teachers fear students will not willingly interact in activities and discussions and therefore must be coerced. It typically advantages certain learning styles and personalities who are good at speaking up. Students who are shy, reflective in their learning style, suffer from a speech disorder, or have previously been embarrassed by wrong answers are only a few examples of those who may be reluctant to participate openly in class discussions.

There are better ways to help students participate. Inviting students to interact through inductive teaching techniques, brainstorming, a Socratic teaching style, listening carefully to and recognizing the value of what each student has to say, and breaking the class into small discussion groups are just a few strategies that will encourage student participation. Teachers who want to avoid being discriminatory as well as embarrassing students should simply eliminate participation from their achievement grade. Some exceptions would be classes such as speech, music, and foreign languages.

Figuring student **effort** into an achievement grade is highly subjective and not related at all to skills or knowledge of the subject. Effort is a behavioral matter and usually denotes motivation and interest in the course content or class activities. If information about student interest, motivation, and effort is important to pass along to those concerned with class achievement, this should be done by using oral or written statements specifically describing behaviors. Using achievement grades to motivate students may appear at first to be professionally responsible; however, when the inflated grade passes along misinformation, it affects the integrity of the communication to the reader.

Improvement is also not relevant to achievement. Improvement implies a change, but it does not provide baseline data or explain to what extent the student improved. However, communicating effort and improvement to students, parents, and interested others is very good feedback. It is often the motivating force behind students setting and reaching higher academic goals. Although this feedback is crucial to students success, it must be communicated by other means than through the achievement grade.

In addition, effort and improvement grades sometimes have the appearance of being inequitable to students. As an example, one of my students related an experience she had with her grade in one of her science classes. She had earned 79 points and received a C, just missing a B in the class by a single point. Her roommate also earned 79 points but received a B.

When she talked to her professor about this inconsistency, he explained to her that her roommate improved more on the second test than she did. The reward for this improvement was the higher grade. The student ended our conversation by reflecting with me "how can anyone with so much education not understand that two students who have the same 79 understanding of the subject should be given the same achievement grade?" The ambiguity and unrelatedness of figuring in improvement is not fair nor is it relevant to student achievement.

Extra-credit coursework would be fair only if it were offered equally to all members of the class at the beginning of the course. Near the end of the grading period, students occasionally will ask for extra-credit assignments or to re-take tests in order to bring up their grades. Unless this opportunity is announced and made available to the whole class, allowing a few students to make up

155

for lost ground would be denying other students an equal opportunity.

When extra-credit assignments are allowed, they should add to student knowledge and skills within the proper context of the course content. They should not involve activities that are not academically relevant, such as grading papers, cleanup activities, or doing errands.

Grading down for **misspelling or poor grammar** in non-language classes poses an interesting contradiction. On one side of the argument is the question of whether all faculty should have the educational responsibility for teaching and requiring good writing skills. The answer, of course, is yes. Writing ability and spelling are important to every student's education and should be monitored by all teaching faculty. The contradiction arises from whether students' poor communication skills should be averaged into the final grade in non-language classes.

Let's use the example of a student who hands in a science paper that is outstanding in every way except for numerous spelling and grammatical errors. Grading down for the language errors would misrepresent the student's understanding of science. But to allow the student to hand in an assignment replete with writing errors would be professionally irresponsible.

The answer is to get away from the thinking that educators need to grade everything they require. Instead of grading down, for example, poorly written papers might be returned for appropriate corrections and accepted only when good writing standards are met. Teachers might want to work cooperatively with the student's writing teacher, who may just be looking for an opportunity to find a subject that will motivate the student to write.

Although these other approaches would meet the immediate need of correcting writing errors, perhaps it should also be made clear that along with mastery of course content, good communication skills will be an expected part of the class rigor and integrated throughout the curriculum. It is very important that students get the message from all their teachers that the ability to communicate well is valued throughout life.

Grades should accurately reflect the **final measure of achievement** in the course. Unsatisfactory coursework at the beginning of the class averaged with demonstrated ability at the end could misrepresent the student's final skill level achieved. For example, in courses such as writing composition or art, figuring in poor grades for early, less successful work would distort the final measure of achievement at the end of the grading period. Professional judgment allows for a more holistic approach to assessment.

And finally, **grading homework**, **papers written outside class**, **portfolios**, and **take-home exams** beg the question of whose work is being graded. This is one of the most frustrating issues teachers face. On the one hand, class time is very limited, and therefore outside time must be used in ways that will enhance student understanding of material. Conversely, as educationally sound as outside assignments are, the work turned in does not necessarily represent valid evidence of individual student achievement.

Homework assignments are inherently unequal. The inequalities within the classroom are numerous enough, but outside the classroom there exists very little equality in educational opportunities. For example, how fair would it be to grade the homework of a student whose home is conducive to study alongside the homework of a student whose homelife is hostile to learning. But in spite of this inherent inequality, many educators do grade homework. Although homework is often not completed for any number of reasons, most of these teachers are convinced that grading is the threat needed to get the work done.

The problem is that grading homework not only fosters cheating, but it has the effect of pushing students out of school. How many students are "sick" or skip class if they do not have their homework completed? How many students copy the work of others or have help from home? How many students are doing their homework in the period before it is due? And who wants to go to class only to be embarassed by teachers making examples of students not completing their homework assignments?

To bring about more equity, as well as more learning, educators must use alternatives to grading homework. Instead of viewing homework as a summation of achievement, for example, it can be used more as a form of practice towards mastery of the subject, similar to someone practicing the piano for their lesson the next day. To illustrate, the following are some ideas that avoid achievement grading and at the same time motivate students to complete outside assignments:

1. Bring up the assignment's due date for class discussion as a way of having students feel responsible for meeting the deadline. When the whole class agrees on a reasonable time for the work to be completed, a lot of weight is shifted from the teacher's shoulders to those of the students.

2. "Busy work" is obvious to students. Teachers could place the responsibility for learning on students by allowing them some authority in the assignment. For example, assign thirty problems and ask students to practice as many as they think they need to understand the concept. This communicates a message to students about the importance of practice to bring about understanding as well as trusting in their ability to assess their own learning.

3. Encourage cooperative efforts among students when doing homework as a way of stimulating interest in the assignment, and suggest peer coaching for students experiencing problems. Parents, siblings, and classmates can provide easily available and often helpful resources.

4. Take time to get students started on homework assignments before they leave class. Sending students home with an assignment they do not understand or do not have the ability to do is very discouraging. When it is started in class, teachers can diagnose potential problems and students get home knowing how to do it, and are often motivated because they have part of their homework already finished.

5. When homework is due, it should be discussed that same day, with each student checking their own work. Not giving proper class time to homework indicates it was not important. Also, exchanging homework with another student violates student confidentiality as well as denying them the best opportunity to get immediate feedback on what they have done.

6. Use homework for diagnostic purposes. It is an excellent way to learn if the teaching methods being used are effective in addition to identifying students experiencing trouble with the material.

7. Approach homework not as something students have to do, but as something they **get to do** to enhance their understanding and experience the joy of learning new knowledge.

Determining whether **term papers** are actually each student's own effort can sometimes be very difficult. Writing style and knowing a student's previous work is helpful, but not always a valid test. The more an assignment requires personal experiences and their own thinking, the less likely students are to solicit outside help. Reflecting understanding is always fundamental to any paper, but requiring personal opinions and conclusions that demonstrate the ability to synthesize and evaluate make plagiarizing much more difficult. The difficulties in determining students' work is also true of **portfolios**. Help from teachers, parents, and helpful friends many times add something to the mix which can misrepresent a student's real abilities.

Take-home exams are used most effectively in smaller classes where teachers have other means of establishing levels of achievement. Much can be learned about students in classes where there is plenty of interaction and individual ability has an opportunity to surface. The take-home exam then becomes more of a culminating activity that summarizes the important aspects of the course and confirms the suspected achievement of individual students.

There are some advantages to take-home tests. They can be more comprehensive than in-class tests, give students as much time as is needed to complete them, and are an educationally sound method of learning subject matter. Because it is common for students in the class to cooperate and help each other, take-home exams are great learning experiences, but they do not always accurately represent the individual understanding of students.

In conclusion, teachers should make every effort to ensure that grades are an accurate reflection of student academic achievements. The balance between the need for educators to use an achievement grade to control behavior and the students' need for accurate assessment must tip in favor of students' liberty interests and their right to future opportunities they have earned.

As a way of making the point again, consider the following metaphors. Is it not true that all pre-operative patients, as they lie waiting for surgery, hope and pray their surgeons' successful completion of medical school was not due to grades inflated by effort and improvement? What would the skydiver be thinking about during the airplane ride if he or she knew the person who packed the parachute graduated from Parachute Packing School because of a good attitude and always being on time. Again, the issue is not what the teacher thinks the grade should mean, but what **those people interpreting the grade** believe it to mean.

Daniel Blaufus, a teacher at Kraxberger Middle School in Gladstone, Oregon, experienced a dramatic change in his classroom as he adopted a more judicious approach to management and grading. The following are his words:

> The most immediate effect of my reading of *Judicious Discipline* is in my classroom management. The entire atmosphere of my class and the relationship I have with my students has been radically changed. My old emphasis of discipline and deadlines has been replaced with compassion, understanding, and the best interest of the individual. It's remarkable to me how much I am suddenly enjoying teaching and how much my students are finding me to be an adult to whom they can turn for understanding. There have been times in my years of teaching when individuals have known that I genuinely care about them as individuals, but with a few alterations in approach, I have one hundred twenty-five kids who feel I am really working for them.
>
> These changes have come about through implementing many of the strategies outlined in *Judicious Discipline*. It has felt so right to tell parents and students that I believe it is important that the course work is completed. When parents come in for explanations of their child's incomplete, my remarks make sense and show profound respect for the student and the subject matter. Every encounter I have had with parents and students has been very positive because the choice is left with them. Not all of them have made up the incompletes, and when the counseling department comes to me to find out what grade the child earned, I give them my best professional assessment of the student's knowledge. I finally feel like a professional educator and not a youth group leader trying to instill all sorts of values and behaviors before I can give a grade.

Punishment

As stated previously, **_Judicious Discipline_** is designed to avoid punishment or the threat of punishment. Punishing students has the effect of diminishing their self-worth and breaking apart the professional student/educator relationship. But because it takes time and practice for many educators to move away from punishing students to a more judicious approach, I have included in this section some discussion of the legal issues and problems surrounding the subject of punishment.

Legal Implications

A legal punishment must begin with a clear perspective of the gravity of the offense. Well-chosen disciplinary measures should be in proportion to the offense and reasonably defensible for the purpose used; i.e., to deter improper conduct, punish, or remove the student. Age, as well as the mental, emotional, or physical condition of the students being punished, are factors that must be considered when determining reasonable punishments. Punishment must never be used in a way that can be construed as malicious, cruel, or excessive.

Teachers should provide oral explanations of the rules listed in student handbooks, ensuring adequate notice has been given of the possible punishment for rule violations. Students have a valid argument when they admit they knew it was against the rules for them to copy another's answers on a test, but were not aware that cheating could result in punishment as severe as expulsion. Punishment as a deterrent or a legal consequence is only as effective as the sufficiency of notice.

Withholding privileges, as opposed to rights, is considered a legal punishment. Students have a right to participate in basic curriculum activities as opposed to those considered "extracurricular." For example, a senior who seriously disrupted the school environment on the eve of graduation has the right to graduate on the basis of having met the requirements, but the privilege of participating in the graduation ceremony may be denied as a reasonable disciplinary measure.

However, denial of an extracurricular activity may not be arbitrary; it must be reasonably related to student behavior.

Corporal punishment has long been used to punish students for unacceptable behavior and, in some states, is still a legal option for administrators who choose to adopt it as school policy. Extreme caution must always be exercised when educators hit or touch students, due to the possibility of violating child abuse laws.

If permitted by state law and authorized by a school district, the administrative procedure related to corporal punishment should include the following:

1. Parental approval;
2. A due process procedure that includes charges, evidence, and the student's right to be heard;
3. Reasonable administration with moderation, prudence and consideration of the gravity of the offense, and physical condition and size of the student;
4. Be privately administered apart from the presence or hearing of other students;
5. Be witnessed by a certificated staff member;
6. Be properly recorded and placed on file as a matter of record;
7. Notification to parents or legal guardian.

Most state laws allow educators to use **reasonable physical force** upon a student when and to the extent an educator reasonably believes it is necessary to maintain order. The situation occasionally occurs when attempting to remove a disruptive student from a class or defending against an attack. Whether reasonable physical force was used is always a question for the jury and will turn upon whether the force employed was necessary and proportionate to the risks presented in each case.

Educators who use **detention, suspension,** or **expulsion** are simply employing society's last resort to misbehavior: the criminal-justice model of incarceration.

There are four basic public interest arguments our government uses to remove criminals from society. They are as follows:

1. To protect society from the criminal. (School rationale: Dangerous students are a menace to everyone and "should not be walking the halls.")
2. To teach criminals a lesson. (School rationale: Students must suffer the consequences of their illegal acts and will thus be deterred from committing offenses in the future.)
3. To teach others a lesson. (School rationale: To be caught and serve detention serves as a deterrent to others who may be thinking about committing an illegal act.)
4. To rehabilitate criminals. (School rationale: Remove disruptive students in order to provide them with skills and attitudes for success when they return to the classroom.)

Problems with Punishment

To **reprimand** students in the presence of their classmates not only has a detrimental effect on their self-concepts, but often intensifies into a spectacle of human emotions and verbal exchanges. Confidentiality and liberty are negated by the public release of professional information and personal feelings.

The irony of **spanking students** is that many who act out in schools come from abusive homes. How is their situation improved if we hit them in school?

Punishing students for the **actions of their parents** or others over whom students have no control leads to feelings of injustice and hopelessness that come from being caught in the middle. For example, students punished because of their parents' refusal to attend disciplinary conferences creates an attitude of confusion and frustration.

Prior to **keeping students after school** as punishment or for any other reason, consider the foreseeable problems related to their transportation and whether they will get home safely.

The embarrassed faces on fidgeting students sitting **outside classroom doors**, sheepishly eyeing those passing by, is a constant reminder of the effect public banishment has on student self-worth. Whenever possible, speak with students privately and avoid the embarrassment caused by the public exercise of authority.

Writing students' **names on a blackboard** can be equally humiliating and have the same psychological effect as spanking students in front of the class or placing them in the hall. In most cases, students whose names are on the board have been tried and convicted by the teacher without their due process rights of notice of the rule they violated, evidence against them, and opportunity to tell their side of the story.

Not allowing students to participate in class because they **do not have their school supplies** is not consistent with their right to an equal educational opportunity. Students have a right to the school supplies necessary for their education. Some teachers allow students to "borrow" materials for class as a way of modeling the importance of student responsibility while still permitting the student the benefit of classroom activities.

Punishing students by **requiring more academic work** discredits the intrinsic value of learning as it undermines the legitimate educational purpose of schools. An example would be a teacher who would say " if you don't stop talking so much I am going to give you a homework assignment tonight." Educators must avoid using subject matter and learning activities as a form of punishment.

It is ironic that the same classrooms used to stimulate and encourage learning are also designated as **detention** rooms to punish misbehaving students. A student doing detention is the same as a prisoner in jail. Although the criminal-justice arguments are often used by educators to justify detention for students, in almost every case they do not work as they were designed. In addition to their ineffectiveness in changing behaviors, they take students away from the learning environment. This is also the problem with in-school suspension. Students in any form of detention are being deprived of an equal educational opportunity. Detention rooms are no more effective than prisons in bringing about positive change, and in some cases they serve as the breeding ground for prison life. Some students misbehave in their first class in order to be with their friends in detention.

I do not recommend punishment in any form. The repercussions are simply antithetical to the goals of professional educators. I recommend mentoring strategies that begin with education and encouragement, proceed through counseling and conferences, and eventually move as a last resort to reassigning students to an alternative educational environment. Observing student responses in each stage will give educators the feedback necessary for appropriate next steps that must be taken.

Property Loss and Damage

Reasonable rules protecting public school property generally make sense to students. If a problem occurs, it is usually because of a lack of communication resulting from whether or not students have received adequate notice that their actions were damaging to school property. For example, students who are allowed to put their feet on chair seats at home may find nothing wrong with doing it at school, or shop students who have not been instructed otherwise might use a chisel as a screwdriver.

Identifying and discussing foreseeable problem areas at the beginning of class will undoubtedly lessen the likelihood of student mis-understanding and embarrassment resulting from lack of information. Adequate notice and proper instruction are essential to a fair and reasonable school policy designed to protect property from loss and damage.

Restitution for damage to school property should be the first Judicious Consequence considered. Putting things back the way they were would certainly be commensurate with any destructive act. An apology to the persons involved would complete the restoration. Public service, for example, has traditionally been accepted by judges as an appropriate lesson for public offenders. A few options educators could discuss with students might be: (1) making "Keep the School Clean" signs for display around school; (2) picking up litter around the school; (3) helping with a community cleanup project; or (4) teaching younger children the value of protecting school and personal property.

It would be logical that **equipment or books not returned** could result in loss of privileges associated with the class or activity. For example, a football jersey not returned at the end of the season would bar the offending student from participation in other extra-curricular activities until it has been returned or paid for.

Often school officials **withhold report cards** from students who damage property or do not pay library fines. Although this is widely practiced and legal in most states, it is questionable educationally because it puts in jeopardy the communication between parents and educators. When there are small amounts of money at issue, threatening the withholding of educational information seems antithetical to professional responsibilities.

167

This subject is discussed in greater detail under "School Records." However, students who have accumulated large debts and refuse to pay could face appearances in small claims court, if the school chooses to pursue the matter through an adversarial process.

The loss or damage of any **student's personal property** is always a matter of concern for public school officials. Students and parents should be informed that bringing personal items to school could result in their loss or damage, many times due to the behavior of others. Educators should also make it clear that every effort will be made to help students care for their belongings, but that there is not adequate supervisory staff to insure the safety of every personal item. A solution for the safe keeping of student property might be depositories designated in the office or in each classroom. Often students bring personal items to school for class projects, "show and tell," for personal expression, or enjoyment during free time.

Rules relating to school and personal property should be perceived by students as guidelines for responsible behavior. This could be done by emphasizing an attitude of pride in the school and respect for the property of others. Class discussions, posters around school, and occasional complimentary statements are just a few things that could be done to help promote an awareness about protecting property. A positive educational approach designed to create a protective and caring attitude among students will, in the long run, be far more effective than threats of punishment for property loss and damage.

Speech and Expression

To write, interpret, and enforce dress and appearance rules is often a frequent source of perplexing management decisions.

Control over student clothing is often attempted with a plethora of rules covering unacceptable appearance, including such attire as: short skirts, long skirts, shorts, short shorts, hats, coats and jackets in class, knicker suits, jump suits, coveralls, frayed trousers or jeans, shirttails outside pants, tie-dyed clothing, tank tops, bare midriffs, plunging necklines, jewelry, clothing with slogans, pictures, or emblems, and, of course, hair—length, style, color, and facial. In addition to unacceptable appearance, schools often mandate that students must wear such clothing as: socks, shoes, shirts, and bras. The problem with using the "exhaustive list" approach is that rules must constantly be rewritten as fads and styles change.

This problem is quite evident with the increased gang activity in some schools. New rules are promulgated, often on-the-spot, banning gang-related appearance and gestures in an effort to control drugs and violence on school grounds. The problem with prohibiting gang dress is that the gang will immediately decide on something else to communicate its membership message. This is not a game administrators can win, and in the long run it proves to be very time consuming.

The most effective approach with gangs is to recognize the issue is one of power. Instead of using school authority to push them out, use it to bring them into the school community. Mario Alba, an administrator at Milwaukie High School in Oregon, brought together the leaders of the Bloods, Crips, 18th Street, and White Supremist gangs along with the student leaders and together agreed on a dress code for the school they could all live with. There has not been a gang problem at the school since. Educators can use the gang problem to build community or to push students out. Shared power is by far the most effective method of working with the gang problem.

Schools need only one broadly written rule communicating the importance of dress and appearance reasonable for an educational environment. The message would be one of trust in students ability to decide what is reasonable appearance in the context of a school setting.

Since a vague or general rule on expression is not adequate notice to suspend, students would not be removed from school until all educational, counseling, and conference avenues have been exhausted. If suspension becomes necessary, notice during a conference that the appearance of the student is clearly unreasonable will provide sufficient legal notice.

Students whom school officials believe are going beyond reasonable bounds of dress or appearance should be handled on an individual basis. A simple opening such as "do you feel that what you are wearing is disruptive to the emotional health of some of our students?" would adroitly place the responsibility on students who are wearing questionable statements on their clothing.

In most situations they willingly open up and are ready to consider such things as the embarrassment it may be causing other students or the "fighting words" that could lead to a serious disruption. By just talking it through, most students are willing to find a resolution to the problem.

But if discourse and reason do not work, another avenue could be pursued. While it is true that students have First Amendment rights of speech in public schools, they do not enjoy those rights in their homes. With this in mind, a good next step in matters of questionable student expression would be to contact the home. Inform the student's parent or guardian that their child's appearance may be deviating from family as well as school values. Encourage them to become involved in the situation. If the parent or guardian agrees and rectifies the problem, the matter is closed.

But if a parent comes to school wearing the same expression on his or her sweatshirt that led to the inquiry, it is time to back off. If the student is expressing statements of his or her family values, it only makes sense to work cooperatively with families on issues of acceptable school appearance. But if in the judgment of the administration the student's appearance is **pervasively vulgar** for the age and maturity of the student body, students and parents should be respectfully informed and the First Amendment right must be denied.

Occasionally students and teachers feel uncomfortable or complain about the actions or appearance of another student. In each case the age and maturity of the student body is a very important consideration. When the behavior is not pervasively vulgar, educators could use that as an opportunity to teach tolerance by helping those who are offended to understand that an individual's expression is valued in the school community. If educators work to understand student expression from a constitutional perspective, they in turn will be better able to help others appreciate our nation's rich cultural diversity and the individual differences among personal and family values in today's society.

A good example was told to me by a teacher about a high school senior who came to school wearing a sweatshirt with the words "Castrate Rapists" printed across the front. She was sent immediately to the office by her first period teacher. During the assistant principal's discussion with the girl, he found that her feelings about this issue were genuine and that this statement was exactly what she wanted to express to others. He arranged a meeting with the classroom teacher and the girl. After hearing the girl talk about how she felt about rapists and what she was trying to do about it, the complaining teacher no longer found the statement objectionable. She wore the sweatshirt for about a week without incident.

Other examples of student speech and expression that are protected in public schools include the right of students not to participate in the Pledge of Allegiance. Students also enjoy the right to read ideas contained in books; this right can be denied in school only if the book in question is judged to be pervasively vulgar. Students who bring their own literature to school, or who

171

display pictures and posters in their lockers, should be given notice that these materials must meet the test of their family values as well as the school's test of pervasive vulgarity.

A good strategy when denying student expression is to use one of the four compelling state interest arguments as a rationale for the rule. Legitimate educational purpose may be the reason to require wearing robes at the graduation ceremony or musical performances, or white shirts and blouses for team members on game day. Health and safety might be a compelling state interest to require students to wear shoes in school or protective gear when participating in certain sports or activities. The mental and emotional health of students is the reason used to limit lewd and indecent expression on clothing as well as offensive speech in and around the school.

Not every form of student speech is protected by the First Amendment; basically, **only ideas are protected**. For example, profane language, indecent gestures, and bigoted statements directed at someone and intended to harass have no protection within the meaning of the Constitution. Also not protected are "fighting words" such as racial epithets and taunting remarks which could lead to a serious disruption. A classroom discussion or school forum would be a good way to help students learn that freedom of speech does not give one license to harass others, while at the same time offering them an opportunity to learn that opinions are encouraged in a democratic community.

Student demonstrations seem to surface periodically, and when they do they usually enjoy a high profile due to the publicity they receive. Because of this notoriety, and the right of students to demonstrate, educators should openly embrace and support this form of expression and do everything necessary to help carry out a nondisruptive and safe demonstration. When students are planning a demonstration, it is a good opportunity to talk with them about their First Amendment rights balanced against their responsibility to use an appropriate time, place, and manner for the event.

A good example is a student demonstration that occurred recently in a local high school in my state, protesting the fact the school had no recognition of Dr. Martin Luther King Day. As the students gathered for a sit-in at the main entrance, school officials responded judiciously as they directed students to leave a path for those using the entrance and asked them not to disrupt classes being held nearby.

The students sat there peaceably for about two periods and then left for their next period class. The principal formed a committee of students and teachers to plan a Dr. Martin Luther King celebration at the school the following year. It was an excellent example of turning a disruptive situation into an opportunity for everybody to learn something about how to act responsibly in a democratic community, a great example of educational leadership.

Educators should encourage a vigorous exchange of ideas by providing bulletin board space in prominent places throughout the school for **free speech activities**. They could begin with a large one near the school entrance as well as one in every classroom. A student committee could be put in charge of keeping the bulletin boards uncluttered and looking out for "fighting words" or pervasively vulgar expressions. A high school social studies teacher told me he had a free speech board for each of his six classes. He said students were seldom late because they wanted to read what other classes were expressing. This proactive approach balances student rights with the school's need to control the reasonable time, place, and manner of student expression.

There is also another good reason to encourage students to express their opinions. Let's use the example of the effect of a single flyer stapled to a bulletin board expressing a bigoted statement directed at a minority group of students. The one

173

statement would have quite an impact on those readers passing by and could possibly have them thinking to themselves "there certainly is a lot of bigotry in this school."

On the other hand, picture that same bigoted statement on a bulletin board filled with other flyers, signs, and posters expressing all sorts of different viewpoints and opinions on all kinds of topics. The effect is quite different. Although the bigoted statement remains, most see it now in a more realistic context and are more likely to be thinking to themselves "there must be a bigot somewhere in this school."

Classroom teachers seeking ways to introduce First Amendment rights to their students could initiate a discussion about the responsibilities that are tied to students talking in class. Using appropriate time, place, and manner and the four compelling state interests, for example, could get students thinking about the proper context for talking.

Educators could bring up discussion questions such as: (1) When would talking disrupt the learning environment? (2) Are there alternatives to raising hands? (3) When would whispering be acceptable? or (4) What about those students who learn better when they have an opportunity to process verbally new information? Students will enjoy their new freedom as they learn to make reasonable decisions relevant to talking in class.

Whereas students have free speech rights in school, educators have a professional responsibility not to instill their personal views upon students. Because of the teacher's position of authority and perceived superior knowledge, impressionable students can be unfairly influenced by educators wearing political buttons or making unwarranted personal remarks in their classrooms. If a student's politics differ from his or her teacher's, for example, loss of respect can ensue, leading possibly to learning and behavioral problems. Instead of wearing the button of one political party, educators could wear the buttons of every political party, expressing as an educator the opinion that good citizenship requires everyone to be actively involved in the democratic process.

Educators should not act precipitously or without serious deliberation on issues of student speech and expression. In the words of the Tinker decision:

> ...in our system, undifferentiated fear or apprehension of disturbance is not enough to overcome the right to freedom of expression. Any departure from absolute regimentation may cause trouble. Any word spoken, in class, in the lunchroom or on the campus, that deviates from the views of another person, may start an argument or cause a disturbance. But our Constitution says we must take this risk; and our history says that it is this sort of freedom—this kind of openness—that is the basis of our hazardous national strength and of the independence and vigor of Americans who grow up and live in the relatively permissive, often disputatious society.

With such an important freedom at stake, educators must take the time to help students learn the responsibility that goes with expressing themselves. And just as important, help those who are provoked and disturbed by certain ideas understand that tolerance must be extended to those who are exercising their constitutional right to speak out. Living in a democracy requires giving even the most repugnant ideas a hearing.

Search and Seizure

Occasionally, educators have reason to search students who are suspected of concealing such things as library books, school equipment, drugs, or the personal property of another student. In most instances, educators just want to recover the property, remove a distracting toy from circulation, or return what was taken to the rightful owner. In the past, some teachers have summarily emptied pockets, opened desks, or cleared out lockers in order to locate missing items. This somewhat heavy-handed approach has now given way to students' rights under the Fourth Amendment that require educators to search for and seize suspected prohibited items in a fair and reasonable manner.

The Fourth Amendment of the United State Constitution forbids "unreasonable searches and seizures" by government officials and provides that warrants "describing the place to be searched, and the persons or things to be seized" can be issued only "upon probable cause." This Amendment is applicable to school situations when a state or federal criminal prosecution based on evidence obtained from school premises and the involvement of school authorities occurs. An illegal search will likely bring into play the exclusionary rule used by courts to exclude evidence illegally seized. Although some courts have applied this rule to school disciplinary procedures, the trend is away from excluding fruits of an illegal search at expulsion hearings.

The process for reasonable searches has been interpreted for public school educators in the United States Supreme Court case of *New Jersey v. T.L.O.,* 105 S.Ct. 733 (1985). Justice White, writing for the majority opinion, analyzed what is reasonable under the Fourth Amendment in a public school situation and found that such a determination requires balancing "the individual's legitimate expectations of privacy and personal security" against "the government's need for effective methods to deal with the breaches of public order." The Court determined that the warrant requirement was "unsuited to the school environment" and held "that school officials need not obtain a warrant before searching a student who is under their authority."

The Court further stated that "the legality of a search of a student should depend simply on the **reasonableness**, under all the circumstances of the search." Reasonableness involves a two-

176

fold inquiry: (1) One must consider whether the action was justified at its inception; and (2) One must determine whether the search as actually conducted was reasonably related in scope to the circumstances that justified the initial interference.

In applying these legal standards, the important question is "...what evidence is relevant and necessary to determine reasonableness?" White's opinion helped answer this question when he stated that "...such evidence need not conclusively prove the ultimate fact in issue, but only have any tendency to make the existence of any fact that is of consequence to the determination of the action more probable or less probable than it would be without the evidence." To meet the first half of this two-fold inquiry, the teacher must have some evidence or reasonable suspicion that a student is hiding or has possession of something prohibited before initiating a search.

For example, to allow an administrator to open all the students' lockers just to "see what might turn up" would be without reasonable cause at its inception and thus be in violation. However, several students who reported to an administrator that they saw a school tape recorder in another student's locker would provide at its inception the reasonable suspicion necessary to make a legal search, regardless of whether or not the recorder was found. In the case of a teacher who found something to be missing during class, a random search of all students before they left the room would be a constitutional infringement on their rights. However, if there is reasonable suspicion that a specific student was concealing the missing item, searching that one student would be legal.

The second part of the two-fold inquiry relates to the scope of the search; or "now that I have reasonable suspicion there may be school property concealed in a student's locker, how far can I take a legal search?" If the recorder is not found in the locker, can a search of the student's car in the parking lot, pockets or purse, or a strip search of the student be carried out?

Scope encompasses the reasonableness of the depth and breadth of the search, which must be plausible and logical in accordance with the circumstances presented. It also is a question about the degree of intrusiveness connected with the search. The highest degree would be a strip search or a drug test—the lowest would be the search of a locker belonging to the school. Therefore, when searching a student's person, a higher degree of suspicion or danger is required than that for searching a car or locker. The Supreme Court also stated that the search should not be "excessively intrusive in light of the age and sex of the student and the nature of the infraction." Reasonable cause at the inception and during the scope of the search will both be weighed carefully when determining the legality of a public school search and seizure.

Although the Fourth Amendment states the government must have "probable cause" to search, the standard that is now applicable to public schools is "reasonable cause," which requires considerably less evidence. By applying a lower standard for educators, the Supreme Court balanced the rights of students against an unreasonable search with the custodial responsibility school officials have for the supervisory and educational demands of public schools.

Students who **refuse a reasonable request** to relinquish something they are concealing must be handled with caution. Wrestling students to the floor in order to search pockets or purses may not only result in injury, but be construed later as unreasonable force. Educators confronted with this situation should not attempt to physically search or seize property, but rely on the assistance of other professionals to conduct the search. As in other confrontations, the best approach to manage uncooperative students might be to bring in their parents or someone who has the student's confidence. In dangerous situations educators should call on the expertise of law enforcement personnel.

Random searches of student lockers and desks are legal if educators can show a compelling state interest to conduct a blanket search. For example, at the end of each semester many school officials conduct searches to locate lost school property as well as clean up such health hazards as spoiled food and spilled drinks. This type of search would clearly fit under the state's interest of maintaining its property. It is very important, however, to advise students there will be these periodic searches and notify them in advance when and for what reasons the searches will occur. This open and straight forward approach not only adds to the integrity of good administrative practice in the eyes of students, but reduces student suspicions that administrators are employing "police state" practices.

Health and safety are compelling state interests that permit a blanket search of all lockers in the event of a bomb threat. If something illegal is found in plain view during an emergency search, it would not be unreasonable for school authorities to seize it. In the case of a clear and present danger, such as a bomb threat, we can all expect our constitutional rights will be denied until the danger has subsided.

Health and safety was used as a compelling state interest to require urinalysis of athletes if they choose to participate in athletics. Athletes high on drugs create a risk not only to themselves, but to all the other participants. In *Venonia School District 47J v. Acton*, 115 S.Ct.2386 (1995), the Court upheld a program of random urinalysis drug testing of student athletes. The Court stated that "...students participating in athletics have even lesser privacy expectations in connection with getting into uniforms, showering, and redressing. Furthermore, by choosing to engage in athletic programs [they] voluntarily subject themselves to a heightened degree of regulation."

Whenever possible **have students present** when conducting the search. If students are not present, educators risk possible accusations of taking something else from a locker or desk, or just invading a student's privacy. When students cannot be present, ask another adult to witness the search. Record the property seized. It is important to leave messages to students when taking their property without their knowledge. Although students may be denied some of their rights of privacy, they do not give up their right to notice.

A common practice in education is **taking student property** which is disruptive or not allowed by school rules. Toys, beepers, walkmans, or new "fads" that come along are occasionally taken and held for the student until the end of the school day. Although these items may be disallowed, educators who confiscate property and do not return it within a reasonable period of time are similarly blameworthy of committing a "tortious taking of another's chattel." Students' personal property should be returned as soon as possible, with the exception of illegal items.

Illegal drugs, firearms, or contraband should be turned over to law enforcement authorities. When this occurs, educators should ask the law enforcement officer for a receipt listing the items submitted. A receipt could protect an educator from the embarrassment of accusations that they kept the student's property for themselves.

Educators should also be **giving receipts to students** when they take their property. Writing a receipt is a powerful message that students' property, no matter how insignificant it may appear to others, is considered important and valuable to both the student and the teacher. Many students identify very closely with their personal effects, and when actions by teachers appear not to respect this attachment, students lose respect for the teacher. Just the assurance that they will have it returned will alleviate the emotional reactions many students experience when parting with something they prize. Giving a receipt to just one student has the effect of saying to all the students that their property as well as their dignity will be respected in this classroom.

Giving receipts for property taken is an excellent way to

communicate respect and the responsibility of authority. A former student of mine reported that until she began giving receipts to her second graders, she had not realized that by taking toys from students she was modeling exactly what she was teaching her students not to do—taking things from others. By issuing receipts, however, she found herself exemplifying respect for the property of others. She reported that it had an immediate affect on how students treated each others' belongings as well as their school books and classroom facilities.

Many secondary teachers have also experienced success when giving receipts. A seventh grade teacher told me that the first receipt he gave was for a package of sunflower seeds. When he handed the student the receipt, the boy turned to the class, held it above his head and said "look what the teacher gave me for a package of sunflower seeds." The students laughed as he showed the receipt to some friends on his way back to his seat. The teacher told me that the student's reaction made him very nervous and unsure that he had done the right thing.

But, the teacher went on to say, when the laughing stopped and the students looked back at him, he suddenly realized that he had just experienced his most significant single interaction with students in seventeen years of teaching. Never had he seen in the eyes of his students the respect that giving a receipt had engendered. Since then he has never had a problem with students bringing inappropriate personal items to class. He finished by telling me that the gesture of respecting a student's personal property also had a positive effect on the whole class-room environment.

Although educators are given wider latitude in student searches than are police, it is not a license to conduct blanket searches or invade the privacy of students. The *T.L.O.* case has provided very clear guidelines and all the authority necessary to manage successfully a safe and secure educational environment. Educators who understand and apply Fourth Amendment concepts judiciously will certainly be creating a learning environment of mutual respect.

Press

The First Amendment freedom of the press clause was set forth to prohibit prior restraint. Simply stated, our government does not have the legal authority to mandate in advance what anyone may or may not publish. However, if a publication injures another, the remedy is a civil action for libel. In addition, publishing material that advocates the violent overthrow of our government or that is obscene may result in a criminal prosecution. Although prior restraint may not be legal, subsequent civil and criminal actions both may supervene the publication and wrongdoing will be decided on the merits of each situation. Therefore, the freedom of the press question that faces public school officials is whether the substantive issue of prior restraint can legally be applied to student publications.

As a general rule, students enjoy only some substantive due process rights in the area of school-sponsored student publications. This is primarily because of their age, impressionability, and the fact that they cannot be held legally liable for what they publish. The school board, in essence, is considered the publisher. As a result, students substantive rights allow for prior restraint by school administrators, but such prior restraint must be reasonably imposed.

The Supreme Court in the case of *Hazelwood School District v. Kuhlmeier*, 108 S.Ct. 562 (1988), used legitimate educational purpose as a rationale for prior restraint of school-sponsored student publications. The Court declared "...we hold that educators do not offend the First Amendment by exercising editorial control over the style and content of student speech in school-sponsored expressive activities so long as their actions are reasonably related to legitimate pedagogical concerns."

In broad dictum, the Court suggested three goals: "That participants learn whatever lessons the activity is designed to teach, that readers and listeners are not exposed to materials that may be inappropriate for their level of maturity, and that the views of the individual speaker are not erroneously attributed to the school."

Although students' substantive due process rights are not co-extensive with those of adults, their procedural due process rights are closely guarded by our nation's courts. To restate briefly, the procedural due process rights of students are notice, a fair hearing, and an appeal. Applied to student press matters, adequate notice means the material not permitted in student publications must be stated in a manner that is clear, concise, and reasonably understood by the students.

A fair hearing means that, in the event of a disagreement, the students' reasons for publication must be heard and considered before the decision is conclusive. Finally, the students have the right to appeal the publication advisor's decision as well as other decisions in the appellate process. Although the law allows reasonable prior restraint, courts show little patience with school authorities who waffle on procedural due process rights in matters of student publications.

Because freedom of the press is such a volatile—and often litigated—area of the law, schools should create a **publication advisory board** for the purpose of promulgating guidelines and serving as an appeal body in the event of student appeals. The membership of such a board could include the student editor, the publications advisor, a student-body representative, a teacher, an administrator, a school board member, and possibly a local newspaper editor.

Any appeal to this advisory board or the school administrator

183

should be heard without delay, preferably within forty-eight hours, to avoid the pretext of administrative delaying tactics. The publication board is only advisory to the building principal's decision, but it offers an informed and politic buffer for many sensitive publication issues that must be decided promptly and fairly.

Publication guidelines should include standards of good journalism, emphasizing technical skills in writing and reporting and a statement encouraging students to express their opinions on relevant issues, in addition to a clear and concise list of prohibited subject matter. Publication rules that prohibit obscenity, profanity, or libel, as well as advertisements that promote products not permitted minors, political endorsements, items demeaning any race, religion, sex, or ethnic group, or material that would cause a substantial disruption of the education process are some specific examples of reasonable prior restraint.

The objective of student publications should be to teach and model the importance of a strong press in a democratic society. For example, a student's editorial criticizing potholes in the parking lot or questioning the quality of the school lunches should be judged on its fairness and accuracy as well as the quality of the author's reporting techniques. An open and above-board discourse of student opinion should be encouraged and viewed by educators as an indicator of a healthy educational environment. If school authorities disagree with the student editor's viewpoint of material presented, they can easily disassociate themselves from the substantive views expressed by inserting a disclaimer in each issue.

The *Hazelwood* case, however, does not apply to all student expression that happens to occur on school grounds, only to school-sponsored or curriculum-related publications. The *Tinker* case's serious disruption standard provides the best guidelines to control "underground" or non-school-sponsored publications. Because off-campus publications represent student expression and not that of the school, the opinions published and distributed must be handled differently. In other words, there is little or no prior restraint by school officials, but there is legal authority to exercise some control over the situation.

A good example would be **off-campus publications** being distributed by students on school grounds. These may be in the form of books, pamphlets, leaflets, or newspapers representing many different ideas and opinions. As with other freedoms, the distribution of these materials may be regulated by a reasonable time, place, and manner, and the content by whether it meets standards appropriate to the age and maturity of the students.

Time, place, and manner regulations can be formulated by using the four compelling state interests as guidelines. For example, stapling or tacking leaflets on walls would damage property, distributing materials during class could be in violation of legitimate educational purpose or serious disruption, passing out material in a crowded hallway could cause a safety problem. As for publications appropriate to age and maturity, passing out highly sensitive or pervasively vulgar material could affect the mental and emotional health of students. Bigoted or "fighting words" could be harassment and could lead to a serious disruption.

By using society's rationale for decisions on publication content and distribution, the personal biases of educators are not as likely to be questioned. It is especially helpful to remain self-assured and poised when talking to students who are upset when they are restrained from disseminating publications they believe they had a constitutional right to distribute. Although students may not always agree with the decision, most will comply with well-informed and fair educators doing their best to balance the school environment and the interests and opinions of their students.

There are two very difficult areas educators must deal with in the distribution of published materials—obscenity and libel. It is clearly within the authority of school officials to ban obscene and libelous publications. However, **obscenity** is not easily defined, and should not be envisaged as "in the eye of the beholder" or as "I know it when I see it." The personal taste of educators should not be the determining factor.

The best language for these guidelines in this area comes from court cases deciding on the merits of many different situations. These guidelines tend to be quite broad in nature, but give us some language we can use when examining the content and explaining our decision to students. The following is an example of these guidelines:

> ...A state offense must be limited to works which, taken as a whole, appeal to the prurient interest in sex, which portray sexual conduct in a patently offensive way, and which, taken as a whole, do not have serious literary, artistic, political, or scientific value. (*Miller v.California*, 413 U.S. 15, 24 [1973])

Prurient interest is a phrase used often in court decisions defining obscenity and is generally interpreted as "having or expressing lustful ideas or desires."

In order for the statement to be **libelous**, it must be more than just false or misleading. It must also cause at least nominal injury to the person libeled, must be malicious, and must be attri-butable to some fault on the part of the person publishing the material. Predicting whether distributed material will be libelous is very difficult, since injury is only speculative. More-over, public figures have higher expectations of false and misleading statements, thereby coming under a higher fault standard.

Public school educators are considered public figures and therefore come under this higher fault standard. Demeaning statements or outlandish caricatures published by students to lampoon authority figures simply must be "taken with a grain of salt" and just be considered as part of the job. Because of its complexity and emotional cost, educators should approach sus-pected matters of libel with caution. If there is a question about the publication, move it up through administrative channels and possibly to the school district's attorney.

And finally, do students have a constitutional right to **pass notes** in class? They are in essence publishing and distributing ideas when they pass notes to one another. By discussing the proper time, place, and manner in which to pass notes in class, teachers have an excellent opportunity to turn a behavior commonly considered disruptive into a positive writing activity, as well as helping students learn the importance of their responsibility to others. The Constitution is given real meaning when something as widespread and enjoyable to students as passing notes is perceived as a matter of civil rights.

In summary, there is a delicate balance between responsible student journalism and students' right to publish. Unreasonable censorship of student publications quickly escalates and is often a feature news item in the local press—and on occasion can attract national attention. The "fourth estate" hangs together very well. The national press vigorously guards its freedom from prior restraint and thirsts to champion even the smallest of publication injustices.

As a consequence, educators should make every effort to avoid confrontations around matters concerning freedom of the press. Educators must make decisions matured by representative publications committees, assign qualified publication advisors, and learn to embrace this fundamental right so important to our nation's heritage.

Religion

The First Amendment to the Constitution provides that "Congress shall make no law respecting an **establishment** of religion, or prohibiting the **free exercise** thereof." When applied to public school settings, this double-edged sword forbids the establishment of religion by school personnel, while at the same time it allows the free exercise of religious practices by students.

In other words, students can freely exercise their religion and educators have the responsibility not to establish theirs. Because teachers' rights flow from school boards, unlike students, they essentially have no free exercise rights in the classroom, although they would have free exercise rights to leave school to engage in their own religious celebrations

For example, students have the right to express their religious beliefs, but educators who wear religious symbols or talk to students about their religious convictions are in effect establishing their own religion. Because of the interpretation of these two clauses, religion in public schools is one of the most difficult and politically volatile issues facing educators today.

It is important, therefore, that educators develop a legal perspective on religious discrimination. The process begins with an understanding of how to apply the tripartite test developed by the Supreme Court over many years and brought together in *Lemon v. Kurtzman*, 403 U.S. 602 (1971). Public school activities must pass three tests if they are to meet the constitutional criterion of nondiscriminatory practices.

First, the activity must have a **secular legislative purpose**. Secular purpose usually translates into legitimate educational purpose, which means religion can be presented in school only in an "educational context." For example, teaching about the part religion played in the early settlements in America would be appropriate in a history class.

Second, its principal or primary effect must be one that **neither advances nor inhibits religion**. In other words, school officials must remain neutral and cannot celebrate or advocate a religious point of view, nor can they take a hostile attitude toward religion or impair its worth.

Third, the activity must not foster an **excessive governmental entanglement** with religion. There must be a real and apparent separation between religion and the public school. Entanglement matters usually involve monitoring activities and control over the use of federal funding and decision-making authority.

The most effective way to meet this tripartite test is to approach religion in public school from an **educational perspective**. References or activities related to religion are constitutional only if they are intended for a legitimate educational purpose. In 1963, Justice Clark's opinion upheld this concept in *Murray v. Curlett*, 374 U.W. 203 (1963). He stated:

> ...it might well be said that one's education is not complete without a study of comparative religion or the history of religion and its relationship to the advancement of civilization. It certainly may be said that the Bible is worthy of study for its literary and historic qualities. Nothing we have said here indicates that such study of the Bible or of religion, when presented objectively as part of a secular program of education, may not be effected consistent with the First Amendment.

It is the educator's responsibility to integrate religion's rich and diverse history, traditions, and doctrines into appropriate subject matter areas. As long as school personnel approach religion from an educational perspective, they will be considered responsible educators and their curricula will be perceived as having a secular legislative purpose.

However, if school activities resemble a religious celebration, or if educators' remarks have the effect of advocating or advancing religious beliefs, then clearly there is a violation of the establishment clause. The line that exists between legitimate educational purpose and religious celebration or advocacy is a fine one, often resting on educators' intentions and the manner and mode of expression.

For example, religious music performed at the "winter concert" may be presented as an entertaining evening of seasonal music representing the educational achievements of students learning to perform before an audience. Christmas carols included in the performance would be presented as "music that Christians sing this time of the year to celebrate the birth of Jesus Christ." Whether such a concert comprises a constitutional infringement is usually "in the eye of the be-holder" and based largely on where the emphasis is placed—be it staging, programming, styling, or the secular or sectarian intent of the director.

School prayer has the appearance of advancing religion through celebration, and for that reason violates the establish-ment clause. School practices include everything from children saying grace before a snack to coaches praying with their teams before a game to an invocation at graduation. The Supreme Court has made it clear that these practices are discriminatory. As a result, many traditions are changing. In place of invocations, for example, many educators have substituted meaningful prose or poetry to open assemblies and other school-wide events.

Although prayer in public schools is unconstitutional, invoca-tions and benedictions in Congress or at city council meetings are not. Prayers in the public sector have been held constitutional only if they are used for a secular legislative purpose. Ceremony, tradition, and its "solemnizing" function are the most common reasons cited for secularizing prayer at public functions, as well as the argument that "it is simply a tolerable acknowledgement of beliefs widely held among the people of this country." But educators must be aware that these legal arguments have yet to be applied to elementary and secondary public schools because of the students' age and impressionability, and the propensity of students to emulate their educators.

Although school-sponsored prayer is discriminatory, a moment of silence for a legitimate educational purpose would be legal. For example, many coaches provide a quiet time before a game for the team to relax or "psych" themselves into playing well. By having a secular purpose for silence and contemplation, coaches or others using this practice are neither advancing nor inhibiting students' free exercise rights to pray silently during this time.

Voluntary student prayer and religious study groups meeting in public secondary schools have in the past been held in many states to be unconstitutional. However, the **Equal Access Act** (EAA) enacted by Congress in 1984 requires that when secondary schools do create limited open forums by allowing noncurriculum related clubs to meet during noninstructional time, they cannot then deny access to school facilities to any group based upon the group's philosophical, political, or religious viewpoints.

The United States Supreme Court decision in *Board of Education of Westside Community Schools v. Mergens*, 496 U.S. 226, upheld the EAA. The Court held that the EAA does not violate the Establishment Clause primarily because the school does not sponsor the religious club, but merely allows it access to school facilities. But in so doing, they narrowed greatly the definition of curricular after-school student organizations. As a result of this new definition, any student group that does not directly relate to the body of courses offered by the school, for instance a chess club, is noncurriculum related. Therefore, a secondary school offering a chess club, or any other noncurriculum-related club, has created a limited open forum.

Because of the entanglement problems associated with the EEA, the Supreme Court's decision narrowing the definition of what is or is not curriculum related, and various state laws which

191

take precedent over the EEA, administrators must work through their school attorney as they draft their policy on students' limited open forums.

The Free Exercise Clause of the First Amendment allows students, with parental permission, **not to participate in classes** or activities that are contrary to their religious beliefs. Although students may be absent from class, working on alternative course work would serve to fulfill the school's legitimate educational purpose. The Theory of Evolution would be an example of curriculum incompatible with the teachings of some religious groups. Although some students may be excused from its study, those who remain should understand that the Theory of Evolution is a scientific theory and not necessarily scientific fact.

Parent-approved **released time programs** for religious instruction off school property for a reasonable period of time each week is constitutional. The Court held that these programs fall within the free exercise clause.

Allowing parochial school students to ride **public school transportation** does not violate the establishment clause, because busing students to school does not advance religion, but only benefits the state's interest in the health and safety of children.

Students **wearing religious dress** are acting within their constitutional rights as they freely exercise their religious beliefs. Students who choose **religious themes** for individual art subjects, wood shop projects, musical solos, composition topics, or term papers are exercising their religious freedoms. When **free time** is provided to students during class time, those who choose to read religious materials brought from home would be exercising their First Amendment rights.

Student-generated **class decorations** for religious purposes should avoid the appearance of being school sponsored. This can be accomplished by providing classroom space at the beginning of

192

the school year specifically allocated for student expression. Also available could be bulletin board space for student expression previously referred to in the section titled "Speech and Expression." Students then could freely exercise their religious beliefs by exhibiting in these free speech places symbols and expressions they choose to bring from home.

I would like to end this section with an anecdote told in my school law class by a Jewish woman whose daughter's fifth grade class voted to make and sell Christmas tree ornaments to defray the costs of their class Christmas party. Not only were many class hours devoted to the project, but the students were told they could sell the ornaments only to family members to prevent soliciting sales from strangers. I still remember how the mother's voice trailed off as she concluded by saying "there really isn't a very big market in a Jewish family for Christmas tree ornaments."

Part of the pain in all aspects of discrimination is the lonely feeling of being "left out." The difference between participating in another's celebration and in a legitimate educational experience can be very subtle to some. But to the one who feels outside and alone, it can mean the difference between enjoying and benefiting from school activities or being "turned off by the system." Not unlike other discriminatory practices, religion can be the source of discipline and learning problems if not handled properly.

Discriminatory Practices

The Fourteenth Amendment, from which all discrimination laws emanate, states in part "...nor deny to any person within its jurisdiction the **equal protection of the laws**." From this brief clause, legislative bodies have enacted enabling legislation that protects students from discrimination based on race, national origin, religion, sex, age, disability, and marital status. In addition, federal and state agencies have promulgated numerous administrative rules that prohibit discrimination. This section is not a review of these many laws, but a brief commentary on how educators' discriminatory practices can affect student attitudes and school discipline.

Whenever educators **emphasize differences among students** it sets up opportunities for these differences to be used in discriminatory ways. Sometimes discrimination is very subtle. For example, elementary teachers often tell students: "It's about time for recess. Let's form two lines at the door, boys in one line and girls in the other." By emphasizing differences in gender just for leaving the room, the teacher is telling students there must be something different about boys and girls for purposes of standing near the door. Conversely, teachers would never think of lining their students up by race, national origin, disability, or religion.

On the other hand, an approach such as "it's about time for recess—let's gather by the door so we can walk together to the playground" serves the same purpose, but does not draw attention to students' gender.

Why, then, do these teachers not see the same discriminatory practices applying to lines based on gender. The answer lies in lack of awareness of problems caused with making distinctions, any distinctions, among students. Even if discrimination is not based on a legally protected classification, it should be avoided. For example, distinguishing among students on the basis of their height, color of hair or eyes, or those first finished with assignments flaunts differences that have nothing to do with the goals of a learning environment.

Educators sensitive to ethnic, cultural, and status issues and who seldom stereotype are more likely to act in ways that result in equal treatment of students. These educators embody qualities that enable them to:

194

Expect the same academic achievement and standards of personal conduct from all students regardless of their ethnic group or cultural tradition.

Avoid comparing or ranking groups with respect to classroom behavior, attitudes, and accomplishments.

Avoid the use of descriptive terms, stereotyped phrases, or participation in humor that is derogatory or demeaning to any group of people.

Promptly admit an error in judgment, sincerely apologize, and be willing to learn new perspectives.

Integrate classroom displays, assignments, and lectures with various people in different roles.

Make seat assignments, work assignments, or play group assignments without regard to race, sex, age, national origin, disabilities, spoken language, marital status, or religion.

Maintain eye contact, smile, stand near, and enjoy all students.

In and around the school or classroom there is always a fair amount of **joking and harassing behavior** that not only affects those who are the target of this humor, but often can create a hostile and anxious learning environment. Whatever the form of or reasons for harassment, the person is being victimized. Students who are the target of such behavior experience illness, loss of confidence, decreased concentration, diminished ambition, and depression. In cases of bigoted taunting and teasing, educators must act immediately by taking an active role in bringing about a resolution. If discriminatory acts are not handled quickly, they are likely to get out of hand.

In addition to harassing language and actions, educators must be conscious of the **appearance of their own classrooms** and offices. Just as with excessive religious symbols and posters that make some students feel uncomfortable about entering the room, the same is true of expressions on any subject matter that might be offensive or in poor taste. Educators' classrooms and offices must be a model of tolerance and sensitivity, not only as an example for others to follow, but to provide a comfortable and respectful place to carry on learning activities. If educators are viewed by all as being resolute in their stand on discrimination, if they are not a part of the problem—respect, appreciation, civil understanding, and tolerance will soon follow.

Classroom celebrations have the effect of discriminating against those who are not celebrating. Celebrating Mother's Day, for example, could make students without mothers feel left out. Valentine's Day makes uncomfortable those who do not have the resources to purchase Valentines, and Halloween pushes out students whose family values find it offensive. The celebrations teachers should be having are those related to a legitimate educational purpose. In other words, schools should be celebrating learning and achievement by including all students as a way of building school community and enhancing the joy of learning.

Often educators rationalize discriminatory practices based simply on the argument that "everyone wants it that way" or that "no one is being hurt." For example, some coaches pray with their players before games because they are all of the same religious background. Or teachers will tell jokes in class demeaning an ethnic group not represented by the students present. In addition to giving credibility to bigotry, these practices violate human rights, due to the fact that **constitutional rights also protect persons not present**. Discriminating against those not there has the effect of keeping students out as well as sending a message that individual differences among those who "stay and suffer" are not valued.

Another phrase commonly used by educators to continue discriminatory practices is the statement "we will do it until someone complains." Although this practice is not legal, the reasoning behind this approach is that the majority wants it this way and only when someone complains will educators have to change and begin complying with the law. "High-handed" approaches can be very intimidating to individuals historically oppressed by the majority. Many parents who would complain are reluctant due to previous experiences in which educators have retaliated against their children in school or they themselves have been branded by educators as being "the problem." When creating democratic learning environments, educators simply must not wait for someone to complain; it is clearly their professional and legal responsibility to ensure compliance with the human rights of students and their families.

Educators who believe in the concepts of **equality** are going to encounter fewer disciplinary problems. Students who feel accepted and understood by those in authority usually have second thoughts about skipping classes or disrupting the educational environment. Educators spend too much time talking and interacting with their classes to think they can deceive their students into thinking they hold attitudes that they do not. Few study educators more, or know their biases and weaknesses better, than their students. Students are keenly aware that the words educators use are only symbols representing what they want others to believe. Words that say one thing while actions indicate another are often the antecedents of putting a student "at risk."

Judicious Discipline requires a genuine commitment and conscientious effort to assure all students an equal opportunity for success. When educators model and teach the qualities of character that make a diverse nation possible, they will have met their professional responsibilities as well as the demands of equity in a culturally diverse society.

Health and Safety

One of the important functions of government is the protection of its citizens. This duty is even more important when government, through its public school personnel, is entrusted with a custodial responsibility for minors. The significance of such matters occasionally surfaces in a lawsuit against the school district, holding those in authority responsible for negligent acts.

While some students may occasionally complain about wearing safety glasses, not being allowed to run in the hallway, or being required to see the school nurse, most recognize the purpose for these rules and, with appropriate reminders, acquiesce. Health and safety policies that are consistently enforced not only protect the students from injury at school but serve to teach good personal habits.

In order to be workable and effective, however, rules governing students' health and safety should be:

1. **Well-planned**—Consider what a reasonably prudent educator would have foreseen under the same or similar circumstances, periodically inspect for hidden dangers, develop a plan to prevent those foreseeable problems, and follow through with its implementation.

2. **Highly Visible**—Use posters, warning signs, verbal reminders, adequate supervision, and other similar measures to insure adequate notice and control over anticipated problem areas.

3. **Fully Understood**—Use instructional handouts,

198

verbal explanations, notification to parents, tests, demonstrated student ability, and other communication efforts to teach students the proper health and safety rules appropriate for the activity.

4. Consistently Enforced—Use proper supervision, be consistent, and don't even let the principal enter the shop area without safety glasses.

As a general rule, there should be a direct relationship between the likelihood of injury and the time devoted to health and safety instructions. For example, a shop teacher who uses power equipment or a coach of a contact sport must set aside considerably more instructional time for safety than a teacher in a regular classroom. In classes and activities where there is a likelihood of injury, the educator should:

1. Provide a handout that details the hazards involved as well as instructions to prevent possible injuries.
2. Discuss, demonstrate, and respond to questions until the written material is understood.
3. Allow students an opportunity to participate and demonstrate their understanding under proper supervision.
4. Make sure all absent students receive the same information and opportunity to participate.
5. Keep accurate records of those who have achieved competence and understanding.

Field trips create the need for even more instruction and concern for proper supervision. Planning for activities off school grounds should take into account the hazards at the site, risks involved in transporting students, the age and maturity of participating students, as well as students with foreseeable problems. Parental notification is essential, not only for legal reasons but also to inform parents about students whereabouts and the educational purpose of the activity.

Liability waivers signed by students and parents declaring their knowledge of the risks involved may be necessary for some field trips and activities. Teachers should inquire of the administration as to the availability and appropriateness of waivers when planning off-campus activities, especially when traveling some distance and with activities that could be dangerous. Using liability waivers is an excellent tool for stating clearly any foreseeable dangers as well as providing some protection to the district in case of an injury.

Schools that allow **students who drive** to use their own cars for school activities should be required to follow reasonable safety rules. This is especially important when carrying other students. Educators responsible for these activities should take the time to check student drivers for (1) a valid driver's license, (2) adequate insurance coverage, (3) good driving record, and (4) written parental permission from all the students involved. By taking these precautions, fewer accidents are likely to occur. And if an accident does happen, educators will appear to have acted in a reasonably prudent manner.

Educators have a legal duty to help students under their supervision who become **sick or injured**. Those who are qualified to administer first aid should do so only up to their level of their expertise, and then proceed to obtain other medical assistance. Those not knowledgeable in first aid should act immediately in getting medical assistance to the student.

If a school-wide plan has been established, educators should act in accordance with the procedures outlined. The importance of following a predetermined plan established by the school cannot be overemphasized. If there is a lawsuit filed as a result of an injury, the educator's actions will be judged on how closely the plan was followed.

If there is a serious injury, educators involved should immediately begin documenting the circumstances that led up to the injury, what occurred at the scene, and any other pertinent information gathered afterward. This information could prove very helpful when an accurate account of the facts becomes important to the attorney representing the school district.

Prudent management practice today would include forming risk-management teams, consulting health officials, staying abreast of literature in the field, attending professional meetings, and seeking legal advice. Educators must anticipate and plan ways to handle foreseeable dangers, carry through with proper supervision and instructions, and be consistent with enforcement. If the rules and decisions are supported by sound professional advice, every effort must be made to hold firm and not waiver in matters of health and safety. Educators cannot afford to compromise the health and safety of students. In addition to the tragedy of a student becoming sick or injured, looming in the background is always the threat of a time-consuming and thorny lawsuit as the result of negligence.

School Fees

Common practice used to require students purchase many of their own school supplies before coming to school each fall. These materials ranged from crayons and notebooks for elementary students to uniform clothing for secondary physical education classes.

However, these requirements changed in the late 1970s, when many state courts began interpreting their state constitutions more strictly with respect to providing for a free public education. Most states followed with legislation that set out what could and could not be required of the families of students.

There has been no consistency among these state laws. Some states distinguish between fees for required and elective courses, and others use curricular and extra-curricular activities as a criterion for exceptions to the rule. Because of this wide diversity, educators must consult their individual state laws to develop their policies on charging students.

Nonetheless, a common thread of unlawful discriminatory practices against disadvantaged families weaves its way through all these state laws. Reasonable rules and decisions sensitive to this issue would be in keeping with the spirit of the applicable state laws. Some suggested guidelines are as follows:

1. Avoid rules that require students to provide any money or materials necessary to meet the basic needs of any class or activity. This would not necessarily rule out allowing parents an opportunity to provide recommended school supplies if they choose.

2. Health and safety as opposed to uniformity in physical education classes should be standard for clothing and towels brought from home. For example, cut-offs are all right but belt loops are a safety hazard and will have to go.

3. School property that becomes the personal property of students may require reasonable reimbursement to the school for materials used in the product. A bird feeder made in wood shop, a garment made in home economics, class rings, annuals, and graduation announcements are examples of products brought home from school.

4. A reasonable rental fee is often charged for the use of

202

school-owned equipment as well as refundable security deposits in the case of textbooks and other materials. Exceptions to paying these fees could be made in the cases of indigent families identified by participation in the federal school lunch program.

5. Many schools charge for student body cards, after-school concerts, plays, field trips, sports, and other activities considered to be extra-curricular. Although this is legal in many states, schools should consider these optional activities educational in nature and make every effort to provide them cost-free to all interested students.

The concept of **equal educational opportunity** is brought home very quickly when something happens as incidentally as a student coming to class without a pencil. Although teachers who would not allow those students to participate usually argue they are "teaching responsibility," the constitutional issue of property and liberty rights would require teachers to find ways for all students to become involved in class learning activities. Students have a right to participate and educators have the responsibility to provide the resources necessary for them to benefit from their equal educational opportunities.

Extra-curricular activities often become the focus of discriminatory practices in many schools. To aspiring cheerleaders or football players, the anticipated expense of shoes alone could be a deterrent if students feel their families cannot afford the investment. In order to offset these discriminatory practices, many advisors and coaches organize money-making activities to defray individual student costs and, in some instances, use donations to pay for those who cannot pay for themselves. While these efforts are certainly within the spirit of equal educational opportunity, they must be handled with discretion.

A graduate student taking my school law class told of a policy in her middle school that required students to pay a fifty cents admission for school assemblies presented during the school day. Those students without the money were assigned to four class-rooms until the assemblies were over, and then returned to classes with the other students. It is not surprising that many of the non-attending students expressed to her feelings of not wanting to come to school on assembly days.

Separating students in a learning community by their ability to pay is not only discriminatory, but it can be a breeding ground for discouragement and despair. While it is good educational practice to provide an opportunity for students to participate in well-planned learning activities and projects, the school activity should not become an end in itself nor a barrier to economically-disadvantaged students whose families cannot afford its price.

School Records

There are laws in each state governing student records. Although these state laws vary widely, the national Family Educational Rights and Privacy Act of 1974 provides well-defined federal guidelines that set forth the rights of students and parents in determining rules and regulations for educational records. In essence, the Act stipulates four major requirements of educational agencies and institutions:

1. They may not have policies that effectively deny parents or eligible students (18 years or older) an opportunity to review and inspect education records.

2. They may not have policies or practices that would

deny parents or eligible students an opportunity to challenge the content of education records believed to be inaccurate, misleading, or in violation of the students' right to privacy.

3. They may not have policies or practices that would permit access to or disclosure of information without consent, unless specifically permitted by the Act.

4. They must notify parents and eligible students of their rights under the Act.

The foreboding shadow of interested parents presents another dimension to the maintenance of school disciplinary records. Until the federal Act, most school records had been available only to professional educators. Because these records are now open to view by parents, guardians, and students at age eighteen, it is even more important that documentation is in fact accurate and free from biased opinion.

Educators must **avoid the use of labels**. Once you label a student, you negate the person. Labels often obscure intended communications, leading to misunderstandings that infringe upon student liberties. Labels should be replaced with statements from first-hand experiences that describe, detail, narrate, illustrate, or characterize student attitudes and behaviors.

For example, a statement that "Bob has sticky fingers" could have more than one meaning. But statements such as "Bob comes to class with sticky fingers on days the school serves cinnamon rolls for lunch" or "I have caught Bob on several occasions stealing pencils from students' desks" are descriptive statements that portray vastly different personal behaviors. Although "sticky fingers" is a label commonly applied to both those who steal and those whose fingers are covered with a sticky substance, the difference between a thief and a messy eater is considerable.

"Susie is lazy." Does this mean she often sleeps in class, does not hand in work on time, is habitually tardy, daydreams, shows lack of interest, does not assume responsibility, or has a learning disability not yet diagnosed? By describing first-hand experiences and allowing others the opportunity to diagnose, educators will not only provide better information to those interpreting it, but legally stand on much safer ground. If Susie alleges some day that the "lazy" label was a detriment to her getting a job or college scholarship, educators will find it far easier to document a history of late arrivals than trying to remember enough examples of her behavior to convince anyone that she was diagnosed correctly as being "lazy."

Administrators should avoid rules that **withhold report cards** from students until a fine is paid, a book found, or a uniform returned. The Family Rights and Privacy Act allows parents access to all records, including the information on report cards. If the parent or guardian has access to a student's record, they are entitled to a copy of it.

Teachers should include progress data only on report cards and restrict behavioral and attitudinal information to parent-teacher conferences. How many ways, for example, could a "U" in citizenship be interpreted by parents whose only source of information was their child's account of the particulars? Personal contact with parents allows for germane responses to good faith questions and an opportunity for proper elaboration of facts essential to successful communication. Information from students' behavioral files should be shared with parents or guardians only in the presence of someone qualified to interpret such behavior. Although it is difficult to contact busy or disinterested parents, educators should make every effort to speak directly with those concerned about student behavior.

Student records simply must be fair, accurate, and confidential in their use. This is far more likely to happen if educators describe in objective terms student behavior and leave labeling to those reading and interpreting the record. When confidentiality has been compromised for expedience, the best interests of students are not being served. Always hanging in the balance are students' liberty interests and future opportunities.

Confidentiality

If there is a vital organ in the body of our Constitution, it is the individual's expectation of privacy from governmental action. There is federal legislation, such as the Family Educational Rights and Privacy Act, and state legislation that provides guidelines protecting the confidentiality of student records and conversations between students and certificated staff. For example, teachers who write names of students on the board for disciplinary reasons are disclosing confidential behavioral information without the consent of students' parents. Not only does putting students names on the board violate federal law, but most states also have laws against the disclosure of students' behavioral records without parental or guardian consent.

Educators in fields directly impacted by the rules and regulations governing confidentiality must be knowledgeable of the applicable federal and state laws. Where these laws do not apply, the principle of professional ethics should prevail. Although ethics do not represent the letter of the law, this sense of professional responsibility and conscience reflects in essence the spirit of our Constitution. The following recommendations have their basis in these fundamental principles:

1. Consider all conversations with students, faculty, and parents to be confidential from others except those who have a demonstrated professional need to know

or if the information involves a serious question of health and safety, i.e., suicide, child abuse, weapons, etc.

2. Take steps to insure that students' academic achievement remains confidential; i.e., code posted grades, use inside or back pages for grades and comments on papers being returned, refrain from verbal comments when returning students' work in class, request permission to display students' papers or art work, etc.

3. Avoid comments and visible reactions relating to student behavior in the presence of others. Holding whispered conversation in a corner of the room or conversing outside the classroom door demonstrates concern for student self-esteem and avoids unforeseen problems related to public disclosures.

4. Refrain from comparing students in the presence of others or putting misbehaving students on display outside the classroom door.

5. Discourage disclosures by others that contain irrelevant and inappropriate information that include confidential data or the private lives of others, i.e., statements made during "show and tell," gossip about students with others, etc.

6. Before touching a student, give thought to possible ramifications, i.e., reactions of abused children, sexual implications, rights to privacy, lawsuits, etc.

Student discipline and academic problems are often directly

related to educators disclosing information that should have been communicated privately or not at all. Often these statements take the form of a flippant remark or sarcastic comment uttered spontaneously in an effort to be entertaining.

For example, telling a student in front of a choir class "you can't carry a tune in a bucket" is hardly the time, place, or manner to diagnose a singing problem. Because of the context of such a remark, and the recognized authority of a music teacher, many students would be discouraged from ever again singing in public.

In attempting to reward good behavior, educators often disclose confidential achievement and behavioral records. For example, a principal recently related to me a problem the school had with a fifth grader who was absent every Monday. Through some probing, she found that every Monday the teacher handed back homework graded over the week-end beginning with the highest grade and moving through the stack to the lowest grade. The student with the attendance problem was always the last to receive his homework assignment. Not only do practices like this violate the law, they affect classroom discipline as well.

Occasionally information disclosed by a student in a confidential relationship gives rise to suspected **child abuse**. Abuse is defined by the laws of each state and generally includes neglect, sexual molestation, physical injury, and, in most states, mental injury or emotional abuse. Despite the fact that the incident was revealed during a confidential communication, the law requires school personnel to report any suspected child abuse to a law enforcement agency or the state agency with the legal authority to investigate the matter.

An abused child is often the result of irrational behavior within the family unit and caution must be used to insure that the focus of the abuse does not shift to an educator blamed by an abuser as the cause of the investigation. Although the law protects the anonymity of the person reporting, good administrative practice would include developing a building guideline for reporting suspected child abuse as well as establishing an effective working relationship with the agency responsible for the investigation.

Consideration of **suicide** and other life-threatening disclosures are examples of confidential communications that must be reported to qualified school authorities. Many student problems are simply beyond the expertise of educators who may become privy to critical situations.

In these cases, one-on-one counseling should be avoided by educators, and the problem directed to those professionals whose responsibility and training enables them to work more effectively with troubled students. This will not only provide better help for the student, but also avoids the possibility of an educator being party to a lawsuit for malpractice.

Educators sometimes hear confessions by students of past or present **criminal activity**, such as possessing or selling drugs, assault, stealing, extortion, and other similar illegal acts. In the case of only knowing about alleged criminal activity, educators are not legally held to disclose the information voluntarily to law enforcement officials. However, educators could be legally implicated as an accessory if they participate in some way after hearing about the crime.

State laws require school personnel to disclose confidential statements of criminal activity if subpoenaed to testify. When students begin disclosing this kind of information, educators must be candid with students by explaining to them about legal responsibilities over which they have no control.

Advising students about abortion, use of contraceptives, conflicts they have with family values, and other similar lifestyle decisions should be carefully avoided. Empathetic listening is, in most cases, very helpful to students working through some of their thinking.

But going further by clarifying values commonly regarded as family issues is a sensitive matter in most communities. Adverse parent reactions, legal ramifications, and students holding the advice blameworthy are possible negative outcomes of imprudent advising of students.

Educators should become familiar with school and community resources that have the expertise and legal authority to respond appropriately to student questions about personal problems.

Students who demand confidentiality as a condition for relating a personal problem are asking educators to compromise their own professional values. If a student says "I have to talk with you right now, but you have to promise me you will not tell anyone else" a professional response should be something like "I cannot promise you that, but I will promise you that if you choose to tell me, I will do everything I can to help you." Most students are looking for someone to help them and are usually more than willing to accept the educator's offer.

Although there may appear to be a fine line between the law and helping troubled students, educators must be able to recognize the difference and stay within legal and ethical limits. Emotional involvement is sometimes difficult to avoid, but educators must convince themselves that they are not the only ones who can solve a student's personal crisis.

Whenever possible, educators should walk troubled students to the counselor's office and introduce them to someone who can be of assistance. Just recommending they see a counselor or giving them directions seldom gets the job done. Distressed students need a clear-thinking professional educator nearby who cares enough and knows how to help them take the first steps toward getting the assistance they need. The personal problems of students are frequently volatile and fraught with unforeseen repercussions. Under very few circumstances would educators want to "go it alone" with students who have serious personal problems.

Although the confidential relationship between students and

211

educators is not commonly associated with student discipline, unprofessional disclosures often precipitate an attitude of mistrust and resentment. On the other hand, educators who ensure an expectancy of privacy are creating a learning environment that lifts and sustains the self-esteem of students.

This confidential relationship gives students a greater sense of security and belonging, which in turn enables them to have a more successful classroom experience.

Complaint Procedures

Casting its shadow over every public rule and decision is the Fourteenth Amendment right of substantive and procedural due process. Whether or not these rights are stated, they are implicit in every public function. How many student handbooks, for example, enumerate the students' process for appeal concluding with the United States Supreme Court? Frequently the rationale of educators is to accord due process a low profile in the hope that students will be less likely to complain if they remain uninformed.

Ironically, the opposite is true. Encouraging student opinion through an accessible and open forum greatly reduces feelings of frustration that are often a cause of discipline problems. For many students and their families, just knowing their opinions will be considered or their grievances heard, gives them a positive feeling about school and assures them that the school has placed a high value on students' rights.

Due process can vary from simply listening to students explain why they were late for class to a formal proceeding involving attorneys, witnesses, and a hearings officer adjudicating findings of fact and conclusions of law. Regardless of the level

212

of the hearing or the expertise of the person conducting it, there are three very important procedural due process aspects essential to a hearing's constitutionality. They are as follows:

1. **Notice**—an oral or written notice of the charges. In other words, the student has a right to know what rule was violated. For example: "You were cheating on the exam."

2. **Evidence**—a summary of the evidence against the student. For example: "Your answers were exactly those of the student sitting next to you."

3. **Defense**—an opportunity for the student to be heard. This is simply an opportunity students to present their side of the story. For example: "We studied together for three nights."

Legally, **complaint procedures** must be specific about who decides what, on what basis it will be determined, and when it will be resolved. For example, if a conflict over classroom rules is discussed first with the classroom teacher, and if a satisfactory resolution is not reached, then the appeal process should state the teacher's immediate supervisor and the actionable time-frames involved. A similar notice of procedure must be followed through to the local board of education.

The school board is the legal entity in every district, with final authority for all rules and decisions. If an appeal is denied by the school board, students may appeal to either a federal or state administrative agency or trial court, then to an appellate court, and finally, if the justices decide to hear the case, to the United States Supreme Court. To restate it simply, every educator's decision has the possibility of being appealed all the way up to the United States Supreme Court.

It is important to remember that the complaint process is a viable one and works best if each step is played out properly and none are bypassed. For example, if a parent complains about a teacher to a member of the school board, the board member should refuse to comment directly on the dissatisfaction and courteously refer the parent to the teacher's principal. Undermining the authority of subordinates can dampen team spirit within the organization as well as diminish student respect for the capabilities of "in-the-trenches" educators.

The **decision on appeal** should be decided without delay and communicated as soon as possible to the parties involved. The longer it takes to make a decision, the more likely it appears educators are "putting students off." When the decision is made, it should be put in writing and, if at all possible, educators should speak personally with the student and parents or guardians. Every effort should be made to be open about decisions and to respond freely and candidly to all questions. A conference with all concerned is good educational practice and has proven to be an effective way to share opinions on sensitive and volatile issues.

Decisions about individual student behavior that affect liberty and property interests are sometimes placed in the hands of **student courts** or brought up to the entire classroom community. There are problems with this practice. A group of students is not very effective at getting to the source of student problems or enabling them to change their attitudes. An example would be a student suffering from abuse at home. He or she does not need the added problems of having personal misconduct scrutinized and ruled on by student peers.

There are also problems associated with confidentiality, with judging the cultural values of other students and their families, with the peer pressure to gossip or be swayed by other students, and with the pressure of making the "right" decision about another student's liberty.

Working out behavior problems should be in the capable

hands of professional educators. Students are far more likely to open up and talk about their personal life with educators than to a group of their peers. The mentoring process is specifically designed for the purpose of helping students resolve problems in a trusting and confidential relationship. Although student input in the formulation of rules and consequences on the first day of class is very important to building community, decisions concerning student misbehavior require the more seasoned, well-informed approach of professional educators.

When educators are "**hearing students out**" there is no particular model that must be followed. Any procedure that is fundamentally fair, and not arbitrary or capricious, is satisfactory. In order to meet the test of "fundamentally fair," an emphasis must be placed on interacting with students in a manner that does not intimidate or threaten, but that encourages honest and forthright responses.

For example, asking students "what seems to be the problem here?" or even the simple question that works every time "what happened?" puts students on notice that something is wrong and at the same time does not stifle good communication. It also allows students to take charge and decide themselves the tone of conversation to follow. In most situations students know what rule they are violating. If it is not clear, educators should take the time to discuss this with students in a non-threatening and helpful manner.

For example, students questioning their grades could be shown an exemplary sample of an essay question written by another student (concealing the name), showing the standard expected for a better grade. Showing examples of good work gets away from defensiveness and lets teachers get to the issue of helping students improve their work.

For our democratic lifestyle to work, schools must take an active part in preparing students to carry out the responsibilities of living in a democracy. Judges, for example, sitting alone in their courtrooms, cannot legally decide whatever issue they choose. Instead, they must wait for someone with legal standing to file a petition seeking a judgment on a question of law or fact. Judges then hear both sides of the issue and decide the question. Until someone complains, the law stands still. For a democratic community to work, its citizens must learn the language of civility and be willing to step forward to exercise their due process rights.

Educators must work to maintain a balance between students' right to adequate notice, a fair hearing, an appeal, and the public's need for an orderly operation of its public schools. The time taken to implement due process procedures sometimes seems to distract from other educational and administrative responsibilities. However, in the long run, the rewards gained for respecting and teaching students their due process rights are endless. It is my sincere hope that *Judicious Discipline* may give impetus to creating democratic school communities that inculcate our nation's highest moral and cultural values—those of freedom, justice, and equality.

HOW ACTION RESEARCH HAS INFORMED THE PRACTICE OF JUDICIOUS DISCIPLINE

BY PAUL GATHERCOAL

How do we know *Judicious Discipline* will do what it says it will do?" This is the question asked of school psychologist, Ginny Nimmo, by her district administrators in Mankato, Minnesota. Ginny and her colleagues were preparing to commit time, energy, and money to implement *Judicious Discipline* in selected schools in her district. Naturally, Ginny's superintendent wanted to know if this move, this paradigm shift, to democratic classroom management practices would actually have a positive effect.

Judicious Discipline professes that **in order for students to become responsible citizens they must be given responsibility**. This notion of giving students responsibility is antithetical to the more practiced theory that responsibility for good citizenship is couched in the educator's power to wield punishment upon wrongdoers and tangibly reward others for their good deeds. From this well-practiced and popular teacher-centered classroom management approach to *Judicious Discipline*, a student-centered, education approach, is one huge, mammoth leap. The leap is so great that some educators will simply not be able to make the shift; and so, schools were chosen to implement this model based on the individual school's culture and the belief that teachers in the chosen schools were ready for such a "leap of faith."

Judicious Discipline operates on the theory that building a school culture through a non-punitive, democratic approach to classroom management and school discipline will produce students who are responsible for their own actions and who will consciously strive to do *good* for societies' sake. It is also claimed that students in schools and classrooms where *Judicious Discipline* is practiced will establish and maintain better interpersonal relationships than students and educators in schools where rewards and punishment or stimulus/response theory is practiced. *Judicious Discipline* argues that there will be a transfer effect of good citizenship at school into the home, the workplace, the sporting field, and to other social settings. Unlike the rewards and punishment models for school/classroom discipline, students' citizenship skills will be transferable from situation to situation. The rewards and punishment models tend to modify behavior for specific situations only; there is no transfer effect. It is claimed that in schools/classrooms where the principles of *Judicious Discipline* are applied educators contribute favorably to students' social development, their sense of autonomy, and help to better prepare them for living and learning in a democratic society.

Driven by her administrators' request for accountability, Ginny approached Paul Gathercoal and asked for help with the research design. Paul developed a research proposal and it was submitted to and approved by the Institutional Review Board (for research on human and animal subjects) at Gustavus Adolphus College. The design was an action research model that employed both quantitative and qualitative measures to test the theoretical outcomes of implementing *Judicious Discipline*. The design also encouraged and enabled the sharing of ideas that emerged as useful models for implementation of *Judicious Discipline* in the research schools and classrooms.

The research results and the models for implementation have been shared widely at conferences and workshops, including the American Educational Research Association's Annual Conventions in 1997, 2000, and 2001, and published in esteemed journals such as the *Phi Delta Kappan* (Landau & Gathercoal, 2000) and the *Kappa Delta Pi Record* (Gathercoal & Crowell, 2000). Some research papers are available online from the Educational Resources Information Center (ERIC) clearinghouses (Gathercoal, 2001; McEwan, Gathercoal, & Nimmo, 1997). As well, several useful implementation resources were generated from the action research findings including the "Conducting Democratic Class Meetings" videotape (Gathercoal & Connolly, 1997) that can be purchased from Corroboree, LLC, 159 Glenbrook Avenue, Camarillo, CA 93010 or ordered online at <http://www.dock.net/gathercoal/Video.html>.

One of the quantitative measures used throughout the five-year research project was a questionnaire developed by The Social Development Group, Research Branch of the South Australian Department of Education, and published in their 1980 book, *Developing the Classroom Group*. This questionnaire was used throughout the action research to ascertain students' levels of social development and provide researchers and subjects with one measure that provides information about the "health and culture" of specific classroom environments.

The researchers found a positive correlation between qualitative measures (videotaped interviews and anecdotes) and the students' responses to the questions on the social development questionnaire. This triangulation of data affirmed the validity and reliability of the questionnaire results; so much so that researchers and teachers began using the quantitative summaries as diagnostic tools to indicate what corrective strategies the educator could take to align classroom management practices more closely with the principles of ***Judicious Discipline***. For example, when the student responses indicated problems with student-student relationships, democratic classroom meetings were recommended and implemented as one strategy the teacher could employ to enhance communication between students and improve student-student relationships.

The social development questionnaire differentiates between power and affect relationships through a series of eight true/false questions and places the student's response in one of four developmental groups "dependent," "rebellion," "cohesion," and "autonomy." The level of students' social development was measured in four categories; two power categories, "teacher power" and "student power," and two relationship categories, "student-student relationships" and "teacher-student relationships." The "teacher power" category represents how much power the teacher held in the classroom versus the student's sense of power. The "student power" category represents how much power individual students felt they had versus other students in the classroom. The "student-student relationships" category represents how well all students get along with each other; and the "teacher-student relationships" category represents how well all students get along with their teacher. So, it was possible for one student to respond at the "dependent" stage for "teacher power," the "rebellion" stage for "student power," the "cohesive" stage for "student/student relationships," and the "autonomous" stage for "teacher-student relationships." Researchers would then score this example as one count for each stage of social development for the individual student. By collecting this information for every student in the school, researchers were able to measure central tendencies and make recommendations for improving the school and classroom culture.

Student behavior for each developmental stage is described in the South Australian Education Department's (1980) book, *Devel-*

oping the Classroom Group, and pertinent passages are reiterated below:

◆ In **stage 1**, the main issue is dependence. Students are generally dependent and submissive, and do what the teacher says. The students' interaction is mostly through the teacher, so there is low covert interaction among students. There is little disruptive behavior, but some "attention getting." Order is fairly high. Anxiety levels are high in some students. Some students are bored. Motivation is extrinsic; approval, praise and encouragement from teacher and parent/caregiver(s) is important. There is fear of punishment.

◆ In **stage 2** the main issue is rebellion. The students test, challenge, and try out the teacher. The student group separates into two camps, one in opposition to the teacher, the other seeking to maintain dependent group behavior. Some students challenge or ignore the teacher's efforts to control the class. Noise level tends to be high. Trust level among students is low, and aggressive interactions and put downs are common. The rebellious subgroup is extrinsically motivated by peer group approval, moderated by fear of teacher punishment. The intrinsic motivation is for autonomy, moderated by dependency needs.

◆ In **stage 3**, the main issue is cohesion. Students are friendly and trusting to each other and the teacher. There is very little disruptive behavior. There is lots of interaction but of an orderly type. They conform to group norms. There is little disagreement, as this is seen as disruptive to the harmony of the group. This inability to handle conflict results in some covert bad feeling. Extrinsic motivation comes from praise and encouragement from peer group and teacher. Breach of class norms brings strong group disapproval.

◆ Autonomy is the main issue at **stage 4**. Individuals are self-directed, able to seek and give support but function well without it. Students take responsibility for their own learning. There is a high level of interaction. Agreement and discussion are the norm; agreement occurs in the context of disagreement. Feelings (positive and negative) are openly expressed. Students work the same with or without the teacher present. Disruptive behavior is virtually non-existent. Students show flexibility and adaptability in a variety of learning situations without demanding conformity of all members. They utilize self-awareness and empathy rather than rules to choose behavior. Motivation is mainly intrinsic. Social behavior is based on respect for self and others. Learning is seen as a way of gaining personal competence and joy. (p. 31 - 35)

Note that the description for Autonomy, or the 4th stage of social development, closely parallels Kohlberg's (1976) fifth stage of moral development (the principled stage or "social contract theory" stage). It was evident to researchers that when classes of students' indicated that they were largely operating at the autonomous stage of social development, the videotaped interviews and anecdotes indicated that those students were also operating at the principled level of moral development.

For example, two kindergarten boys were playing with a bin full of *Hot Wheels* cars when one boy declared, "This car belongs to me, it looks like the other one [that is here], but this one belongs to me. I brought it from home."

The other kindergartener asks, "Are you sure this isn't a property issue?"

"No I brought this one from home, it's mine."

After a little more play time, the questioning kindergartner says, "I'll tell you what, let's line all these cars up and you can put yours next to the one that it looks like."

The other kindergartner quickly back-peddles with, "Oh, maybe this isn't mine, but it looks just like mine." Not a problem, as five-year-olds use social contract theory and the language of civility to solve a property issue.

Another example finds a fourth grader telling what she knows about *Judicious Discipline* on videotape,

> I know that it helps us keep a clear balance on everything that happens and that everyone has rights in the *Judicious Discipline*. Um, everywhere you go there is this *Judicious Discipline* and we are always reminded about it. Um, if someone is not acting in the *Judicious Discipline* way or taking responsibilities, they are reminded, usually. Um, let's see, that everyone has to respect everyone else's rights and take the responsibilities of that. I know that having the *Judicious Discipline* means I have rights and responsibilities.

Doesn't this sound like respect for the rights, life, and dignity of all persons? (Kohlberg, 1976).

Still other fifth graders commented on videotape,

> Everyone has a positive attitude in our class because everyone feels like their opinion is, is like okay to have one and stuff. And we talk out all our problems and we compromise on everything and we're really good about respecting other's feelings and stuff.

> You don't get in trouble for no reason, like sometimes someone might tell on you cause they think that you did something and you didn't, so [the teacher] talks to you and she believes you if you say that you didn't or something.

> And with the rights and responsibilities we all wrote 'em down

and we all had to sign the sheet and then we made some rights and responsibilities for [our teacher] and she had to sign that sheet.

Uh-huh, and so for the most part everyone follows their rights and responsibilities.

This sounds a lot like Kohlberg's (1976) principled level, and the awareness that particular moral or social rules are social contracts, arrived at through democratic reconciliation of differing viewpoints and they are open to change, within principle.

Researchers found it fascinating how the qualitative findings tended to match the quantitative central tendencies found by administering the social development questionnaire to classroom groups. The students cited above all came from classrooms where autonomy or social development stage 4 was the primary response on the social development questionnaire. When students from classrooms where the central tendency response was at social development stage 1 or the dependent stage were interviewed on videotape, there was silence as students sat dumbfounded when asked open-ended questions about rights and responsibilities, respect and justice. Those students simply did not have the language to know where to begin to talk about rights, or what their responsibilities were, or comment on respect or what was fair and right. There was a noticeable qualitative difference between these student's interviews, marked by a distinct inability to respond to open-ended questions, and the language displayed in the interviews with students who had been taught about *Judicious Discipline*, and that are quoted above.

Generally, the schools implementing *Judicious Discipline* found success, but it did not occur over night. Implementing *Judicious Discipline* takes time. *Judicious Discipline* is *front-loading*; you can't just jump in and use it. The teacher has to teach *Judicious Discipline* to his or her students. Students need to know and practice the language and concepts embedded in ***Judicious Discipline***, and they must develop their own expectations for civil living around the framework of democracy, or the balance of individual rights and the rights and interests of the rest of society. Our research indicates that this usually takes between four to eight weeks, if students are learning about ***Judicious Discipline*** for the first time. However, if the entire school is using ***Judicious Discipline***, that time can be reduced to zero as students come to school expecting the ***Judicious Discipline*** model to be in place when they get there. This is illustrated in the following table, as one elementary school where the social development questionnaire was administered to all students five times, over a five-year period, continued to make progress, virtually beginning where they had ended each time the questionnaire was administered.

Unseen in the following table, but evident to researchers, was a distinct difference in student responses at various grade levels. The data indicated that the "early adopters" were the upper grades and the lower grades came later. Qualitative data indicated that lower grade teachers thought that their students would never be able to do ***Judicious Discipline***. Again, this substantiates the treatise that moving to ***Judicious Discipline*** is truly a paradigm shift for many teachers. Nonetheless, at the end of five years, every classroom in the elementary school, except one, scored high at the autonomous stage of social development in all four categories, two power and two relationships categories. This tends to dismiss the myth that the lower grades "can't do ***Judicious Discipline***." Maybe it is the teacher's beliefs and not the students' abilities that impede the process?

Table 1 provides the distribution of responses at the various levels of social development (dependency, rebellion, cohesion, and autonomy). The reported "N" indicates the number of responses that were given by all students answering at a particular stage of social development for the four constructs (teacher power, student power, student-student relationship, and teacher-student relationship). As a result the reported "N" is four times the population of the school.

Table 1.
School-wide Results
for the Elementary School's Questionnaires

Questionnaire #1 - Administered to All Students in September 1995

Dependency	Rebellion	Cohesion	Autonomy
N = 449: 26%	N = 68: 4%	N = 736: 42%	N = 498: 28%

Questionnaire #2 - Administered to All Students in January 1996

Dependency	Rebellion	Cohesion	Autonomy
N = 335: 20%	N = 179: 10%	N = 570: 34%	N = 602: 36%

Questionnaire #3 - Administered to All Students in May 1996

Dependency	Rebellion	Cohesion	Autonomy
N = 284: 17%	N = 129: 8%	N = 510: 31%	N = 742: 45%

Questionnaire #4 - Administered to All Students in October 1999

Dependency	Rebellion	Cohesion	Autonomy
N = 122: 9%	N = 169: 13%	N = 419: 32%	N = 602: 46%

Questionnaire #5 - Administered to All Students in June 2000

Dependency	Rebellion	Cohesion	Autonomy
N = 101: 8%	N = 139: 11%	N = 280: 22%	N = 748: 59%

Note the increase in responses at the autonomous level and the decrease in responses at the dependency level over the five-year period. This is exactly what should happen if a school's culture is truly shifting from a teacher-centered, autocratic form of classroom management to a student-centered, democratic form of classroom management. Qualitative data (anecdotes, videotaped interviews with teachers, students, and administrators, and other artifacts) all support the questionnaires' results indicating a shift from teacher-centered classroom to students taking responsibility for their behavior and civic responsibilities, including learning.

In another fifth- and sixth-grade-only school, approximately 300 students in twelve distinct homerooms informed researchers of the value and need for conducting democratic class meetings. A comparison of central tendencies on students' social development questionnaires indicated that two teachers who conducted democratic class meetings in their homerooms maintained a classroom climate that was more aligned with *Judicious Discipline* than did the ten teachers who did not conduct democratic class meetings.

We found that, in September 1995, students in all homerooms were probably similar in their stages of social development. The results for September 1995 are presented in Table 2. The reported "N" indicates the number of responses that were given by all students answering at a particular stage of social development for the four constructs (teacher power, student power, student-student relationship, and teacher-student relationship). As a result the reported "N" is four times the population of the students in the class.

Table 2.
Results of Student Responses to Questionnaires in September

Teachers Who Conducted Democratic Class Meetings
(September 1995 Questionnaire Results)

Dependent	Rebellion	Cohesive	Autonomous
N = 76: 37%	N = 20: 10%	N = 54: 26%	N = 54: 26%

Teachers Who Did Not Conduct Democratic Class Meetings
(September 1995 Questionnaire Results)

Dependent	Rebellion	Cohesive	Autonomous
N = 412: 40%	N = 145: 14%	N = 248: 24%	N = 223: 22%

Note that there are no significant differences between the groups in September. By February, differences in questionnaire results began to emerge and qualitative data indicated that students who were involved in democratic class meetings felt more empowered and felt more of a sense of belonging to the group. The February results indicate that while the school is making good progress in the area of social development, the two teachers who conduct democratic class meetings are making great progress. The results for February 1996 are presented in Table 3. The reported "N" indicates the number of responses that were given by all students answering at a particular stage of social development for the four constructs (teacher power, student power, student-student relationship, and teacher-student relationship). As a result the reported "N" is four times the population of the students in the class.

Table 3.
Results of Student Responses to Questionnaires in February

Teachers Who Conducted Democratic Class Meetings
(February 1996 Questionnaire Results)

Dependent	Rebellion	Cohesive	Autonomous
N = 11: 6%	N = 19: 10%	N = 18: 9%	N = 148: 76%

Teachers Who Did Not Conduct Democratic Class Meetings
(February 1996 Questionnaire Results)

Dependent	Rebellion	Cohesive	Autonomous
N = 170: 17%	N = 224: 23%	N = 193: 20%	N = 399: 40%

Note, too, that the responses for rebellion are twice as high in the teachers who did not conduct democratic class meetings than the teachers who did conduct democratic class meetings. Qualitative data indicated that conducting democratic class meetings was a way that students could vent their concerns and question authority in a way that did much to reduce problem social situations and quickly led students through the rebellion stage to the cohesive stage.

The May questionnaire results continue to show that the two teachers who conducted democratic class meetings maintained high autonomous level response rates and the ten teachers who **did not** conduct democratic class meetings continued to score very high in the rebellion stage of social development. The results for May 1996 are presented in Table 4. The reported "N" indicates the number of responses that were given by all students answering at a particular stage of social development for the four constructs (teacher power, student power, student/student relationship, and teacher/student relationship). As a result the reported "N" is four times the population of the students in the class.

Table 4.
Results of Student Responses to Questionnaires in May

Teachers Who Conducted Democratic Class Meetings
(May 1996 Questionnaire Results)

Dependent	Rebellion	Cohesive	Autonomous
N = 11: 6%	N = 11: 6%	N = 28: 14%	N = 150: 75%

Teachers Who Did Not Conduct Democratic Class Meetings
(May 1996 Questionnaire Results)

Dependent	Rebellion	Cohesive	Autonomous
N = 158: 16%	N = 268: 27%	N = 182: 18%	N = 383: 37%

These results and complementary qualitative findings support the need for conducting democratic class meetings when implementing *Judicious Discipline*. The elements for conducting democratic class meetings (See Chapter 4, pages 102-106) were gleaned from interviews with students and teachers who through trial and error found strategies that worked best for them when conducting democratic class meetings.

There is no "right way" to conduct a democratic class meeting. The data indicates that successful democratic class meetings can take many different forms and the "best" organization and structure for any class will probably emerge as the academic year progresses. Nonetheless, some elements that work well to facilitate and democratize class meetings did emerge as "key elements" for success.

Educators are well advised to include democratic class meetings in their repertoire of teaching strategies when they implement the principles of *Judicious Discipline*. As educators shift from autocratic class management practices to a more democratic style of administration, it serves educators and their students well to have the key elements for conducting democratic class meetings in place. When democratic class meetings are conducted, in concert with the practice of *Judicious Discipline*, educators can feel proud that they are truly preparing tomorrow's citizens for living and learning in a democratic, free society.

The findings of five years of action research suggest that teachers need to take the time to teach students about *Judicious Discipline*. Teachers who take the time to teach about and practice *Judicious Discipline* in their classrooms reap many benefits. Students in their classrooms are more likely to respond on the social development questionnaire at the autonomous stage, and as a result, these teachers are less likely to feel frustrated and/or experience high levels of work-related stress. Our research indicates that educators who practiced *Judicious Discipline*, ostensibly as it is designed to be used, were respected by others and they taught their students respect by giving them respect; these teachers were "models of respect." These educators indicated that using *Judicious Discipline* gave them feelings of professionalism they had not experienced before. They felt that they were using management strategies that were legal, ethical, and educationally sound. In teaching about *Judicious Discipline* and providing students with a "language of civility," educators found common ground for discussing, mediating and reconciling social problems that developed as a result of living and learning in a democratic classroom/school. As well, students who learned about *Judicious Discipline* were able to use "the language of civility" to advocate for themselves and to use it to solve their own social problems. Students with Downs Syndrome were able to learn the language and respond to its use as a modifier of inappropriate behavior and as a reminder of socially appropriate behavior. Students with emotional and behavioral disorders were treated with respect, and the result was learning the concepts of conflict resolution and a language to help them in the school community and future society.

In classrooms where teachers **did not** spend adequate time teaching about *Judicious Discipline*, or conducting democratic class meetings, researchers found that educators and students had less than healthy student-student relationships and teacher-student relationships tended to be adversarial. Students' responses on the social development questionnaires indicated they were operating at the lower stages of social development. This was also evident in student interactions in unstructured settings, and evident in the large number and kinds of student referrals to the school counselor and the large number and kinds of referrals for assessment by special educators.

One delightful finding was that teachers who used *Judicious Discipline* ostensibly as it is supposed to be practiced indicated lower levels of work-related stress than those who did not practice *Judicious Discipline*. During videotaped interviews with teachers and administrators, when asked the open-ended question, "How's your stress level?," those who practiced *Judicious Discipline* invariably responded, "*Judicious Discipline* has lowered my stress level." The respondents marked the time when their stress was reduced by the time they "took up" using

Judicious Discipline. Teachers who were in classrooms where *Judicious Discipline* was poorly implemented or not used at all simply reported, "Teaching is very stressful." Those subjects noted no quality of difference in their stress level. If there is one good reason to use *Judicious Discipline*, it is that it will probably lower an educator's work-related stress level.

Finally, a word of caution. *Judicious Discipline* is antithetical to the beliefs of those who practice stimulus/response theory in schools and honestly think that students can be controlled with rewards and punishment. Educators who use *Judicious Discipline* well need to be mindful of the effect their performance and advocacy for individual rights and responsibilities will have on those "in that other camp." Our research found instances where educators were literally "pushed out" of their schools because of their advocacy for and use of *Judicious Discipline*. *Judicious Discipline* is "powerful stuff" and when one truly understands the principles, some of our past educational practices and those of our colleagues become laughable in light of finally knowing what it is to be a professional educator. Our research indicates that educators should tread easy on this road to *Judicious Discipline*. Never embarrass your colleagues and never be too zealous in your advocacy. Prepare yourself to be identified as different from other educators. Maintain your principles and seek out educators with similar philosophies of discipline for support and counsel.

Students, too, quickly know that things are different when they come in contact with teachers who use *Judicious Discipline*. As two fifth grade boys remark,

"You know, I mean anything that you might have had in the past besides judicial discipline, it will not be as fair or as good as it would be if you had judic…judicial discipline!"
"Judicious Discipline!"
"Judicious Discipline!"
"It's good, it helps you solve your problems instead of

making you wake up and think about your punishment, instead of what you did wrong."

"Because a lot of the times, like in my old school, when I got in trouble I wouldn't, I wouldn't think as much about what I did wrong. I'd think more about the punishment, because they wouldn't stop to talk to you, they'd just say [taps his finger on the table], there you go, that's your punishment."

"Yeah."

"And they wouldn't say anything about, they wouldn't ask me why I did it. They wouldn't ask me what I might do in the future to solve it, they'd just say, there you go, that's your punishment."

These same boys, when asked what they would do if they moved somewhere else and *Judicious Discipline* wasn't practiced, responded that they would "teach them about it." This sentiment was expressed over and over again in other videotape interviews. Students felt so strongly about the use of *Judicious Discipline* that they said they would teach others about it.

Judicious Discipline did much to establish a new school culture in some schools. It provided all students, educators, administrators, and staff with a common language of civility that was used to solve social problems and think about what was "right" and "good." As Langer (1989) reminds us in her book, *Mindfulness*, "Our perceptions and interpretations influence the way our bodies respond. *When the "mind" is in a context, the "body" is necessarily also in that context.* To achieve a different physiological state, sometimes what we need to do is to place the mind in another context" (p.177).

Practicing *Judicious Discipline* helps everyone to construct a context that they perceive as fair, free, and caring. When we truly believe that this is the state of our environment, we are more likely to think of ourselves as having value; and as a result, we will be less likely to act out against people and things in that environment.

233

It makes sense to speculate, that teachers who use ***Judicious Discipline*** are less likely to be victims of revenge, as their students will be less likely to act out. This is important when you consider that some, not many, but some students are like these kinds of people:

> ...signs of irrational thinking are usually absent. They are egocentric and lack the capacity to feel empathy and love. They have little or no conscience or sense of guilt, tend to project blame when they get into trouble. They are unreliable, untruthful, and insincere, but they are often convincing because they believe their own lies. There is a vast gulf between what they say and what they do. They are impulsive, the whim of the moment being paramount. They are given to periodic and often senseless antisocial behavior, which may be either aggressive or passive and parasitic. (p. 310)

This is the description of the violent psychopath from Restak's (1988) book, *The Mind*. No model for discipline will work well with the violent psychopath. The violent psychopath is not "normal." Yet, the violent psychopath does exist and does go to school. When dealing with the violent psychopath, using ***Judicious Discipline*** probably won't make things worse, and ***Judicious Discipline*** has the potential to make things better. On the other hand, using rewards and punishment (stimulus/response theory) with the violent psychopath could make things a lot worse for all concerned.

The teacher who uses ***Judicious Discipline*** avoids power struggles and encourages students to be responsible for their actions. The teacher remains on the same side as the student and is rarely viewed by the student as the problem or the adversary. The teacher remains student-centered. The teacher maintains the role of mentor and guide when the student is in trouble. The teacher remains ever the educator, armed with knowledgeable resources for teaching and learning. The teacher embraces student behavior problems as a "teachable moment"—another opportunity to teach about what is "right" and what is "good." When educators make that paradigm shift, that philosophical and cognitive leap to *Judicious Discipline*, they feel proud and happy every time a student calls out, "Teacher!"

References

Busse, N. (March, 1999). I can't keep them safe. *American School Board Journal*. <http://www.asbj.com/security/contents/0399busse.html>.

Dreikurs, R. (1957). *Psychology in the classroom*. New York: Harper & Row.

Education Department of South Australia (1980). *Developing the classroom group: A manual for the inservice trainer*. Report No. 4. Adelaide, South Australia: Government Printer of South Australia.

Gathercoal, F. (1997). *Judicious discipline*, 4th Ed. San Francisco, CA: Caddo Gap Press.

Gathercoal, F. (1998). Judicious discipline. <http://www.dock.net/gathercoal/judicious_discipline.html>.

Gathercoal, P. (2001). Conducting democratic class meetings. School Violence and Conflict Programs, Paper Presentation. Paper presented at the Annual Meeting of the American Educational Research Association (New Orleans, LA, April 24-28, 2000). (ED442736). (Clearinghouse: SO031926).

Gathercoal, P. & Crowell, R. (2000). Judicious discipline. *Kappa Delta Pi Record, 36*(4), 173-177.

Gathercoal, P. (1998). Educational leadership and judicious discipline, *Educational Leadership and Administration: Teaching and Program Development, 10*(Fall), 47-59.

Gathercoal, P. (1999). Judicious discipline and neuroscience: Constructing a neurological rationale for democracy in the classroom. In B.M. Landau (Ed.), *Practicing judicious discipline: An educator's guide to a democratic classroom* (3rd ed.) San Francisco, CA: Caddo Gap Press.

Paul Gathercoal

Gathercoal, P & Connolly, J. (1997). *Conducting democratic class meetings*, video. Corroboree, LLC. Available: 159 Glenbrook Avenue, Camarillo, CA 93010.

Kohlberg, L. (1976). Moral stages and moralization: The cognitive-developmental approach. In T. Lickora (Ed.). *Moral development and behavior*. New York: Holt, Rinehart & Winston.

Landau, B. & Gathercoal, P. (2000). Creating peaceful classrooms: *Judicious discipline* and class meetings. *Phi Delta Kappan, 81*(6), 450-454.

Landau, B. (Ed.) (1999). *Practicing judicious discipline*. 3rd Ed. San Francisco, CA: Caddo Gap.

Langer, E. (1989). *Mindfulness*. Reading, MA: Addison-Wesley.

McEwan, B., Gathercoal, P. & Nimmo, V. (1999). Application of judicious discipline: A common language for classroom management. In H.J. Freiberg (Ed.), *Beyond behaviorism: Changing the classroom management paradigm*. Boston, MA: Allyn & Bacon.

McEwan, B., Gathercoal, P. & Nimmo, V. (1997). An examination of the applications of constitutional concepts as an approach to classroom management: Four studies of *Judicious Discipline* in various classroom settings. Paper presented at the Annual Meeting of the American Educational Research Association (Chicago, IL, March 24-28, 1997). (ED418031)

McEwan, B. (1990). Review. Judicious discipline. *Democracy and Education, 4*(3), 37-40.

Restak, R. (1988). *The mind*. New York: Bantam Books.

Sarason, S. (1990). *The predictable failure of educational reform*. San Francisco, CA: Jossey-Bass.

Wolfgang, C. (1995). *Solving discipline problems: Methods and models for today's teachers*. Boston, MA: Allyn & Bacon.

ABOUT
THE AUTHORS

F **orrest Gathercoal** is a professor emeritus with the School of Education at Oregon State University, Corvallis, and an adjunct professor at Lewis and Clark College in Portland. He teaches educational psychology and school law, conducts workshops on civil rights and school discipline, presents frequently at educational conferences, and serves as a consultant to school districts, state education agencies, and colleges and universities across the United States.

Previously, at the public school level, Forrest has been a 6th through 12th grade music teacher, elementary and secondary school counselor, coach, and high school vice-principal. While at Oregon State University, he has been a faculty member in the Department of Educational Foundations and assistant dean of the School of Education.

Forrest holds two degrees from the University of Oregon, a bachelor's in music and a J.D. from the School of Law.

In addition to *Judicious Discipline*, Forrest is author of *A Judicious Philosophy for School Support Personnel, Judicious Parenting,* and *Judicious Leadership for Residence Hall Living,* co-author of *Legal Issues for Industrial Educators,* and author of numerous journal articles and book chapters on educational discipline and school law.

Paul Gathercoal, Forrest's brother, is an associate professor

237

and director of the Educational Technology Specialization in Curriculum and Instruction with the School of Education at California Lutheran University in Thousand Oaks, California. Previously he has served as an assistant professor of education at Gustavus Adolphus College in St. Peter, Minnesota, and as a teacher with the South Australian Education Department.

Paul holds a B.S. degree in education from Southern Oregon College and M.A. and Ph.D. degrees in education from the University of Oregon. He is the author or co-author of numerous articles and conference presentations on educational technology, class meetings, and *Judicious Discipline*, among other educational topics.

BOOKS AND RESOURCES ABOUT JUDICIOUS DISCIPLINE

The following books describing and utilizing the concepts of *Judicious Discipline* are available from Caddo Gap Press:

Judicious Discipline by Forrest Gathercoal, Fifth Edition, 2001, 240 pages, paper, ISBN 1-880192-39-X, $24.95.

Practicing Judicious Discipline: An Educator's Guide to a Democratic Classroom edited by Barbara McEwan Landau, Third Edition, 1999, 224 pages, paper, 8-1/2x11 format, ISBN 1-880192-29-2, $24.95.

A Judicious Philosophy for School Support Personnel by Forrest Gathercoal, 1996, 80 pages, paper, ISBN 1-880192-16-0, $12.95.

Judicious Parenting by Forrest Gathercoal, 1992, 212 pages, paper, ISBN 1-880192-03-9, $14.95.

These books may be ordered from Caddo Gap Press, 3145 Geary Boulevard, Suite 275, San Francisco, California 94118, telephone 415/392-1911, fax 415/956-3702, e-mail <caddogap@aol.com>.

There is also available a 25-minute videotape entitled *Introducing Judicious Discipline*. In addition to a presentation of the main principles, it features practicing teachers and school administrators talking about and using the concepts in their classrooms and schools. For information on how to acquire this videotape, contact the Communications Media Center, Oregon State University, Corvallis, Oregon 97331 or call 503/737-2121.

Also available is an excellent videotape produced by Paul Gathercoal entitled *Conducting Democratic Classroom Meetings*, which is very helpful to educators practicing **_Judicious Discipline_**. For information on ordering this videotape, contact Paul Gathercoal, 159 Glenbrook Avenue, Camarillo, California 93010.